'S COLLEGE

Quality
and Excellence
in Human Services

THE WILEY SERIES IN CLINICAL PSYCHOLOGY

Series Editor

J. Mark G. Williams	*Department of Psychology, University College of North Wales, Bangor, UK*
Paul Dickens	Quality and Excellence in Human Services
	Further titles in preparation

PAUL DICKENS
Royal Scottish National Hospital and Community NHS Trust

Quality and Excellence in Human Services

JOHN WILEY & SONS

Chichester · New York · Brisbane · Toronto · Singapore

Other Wiley Editorial Offices

John Wiley & Sons, Inc., 605 Third Avenue,
New York, NY 10158–0012, USA

Jacaranda Wiley Ltd, 33 Park Road, Milton,
Queensland 4064, Australia

John Wiley & Sons (Canada) Ltd, 22 Worcester Road,
Rexdale, Ontario M9W 1L1, Canada

John Wiley & Sons (SEA) Pte Ltd, 37 Jalan Pemimpin #05-04,
Block B, Union Industrial Building, Singapore 2057

Library of Congress Cataloging-in-Publication Data

Dickens, Paul
    Quality and excellence in human services / Paul Dickens.
        p.   cm. — (The Wiley series in clinical psychology)
    Includes bibliographical references (p.   ) and index.
    ISBN 0-471-94054-2 (pbk.)
    1. Human services.   2. Total quality management.   I. Title.
    II. Series.
    HV31.D63   1994
    361'.0068'5 — dc20   93–36190
                                                                     CIP

British Library Cataloguing in Publication Data

A catalogue record for this book is available from the British Library

ISBN 0-471-94054-2 (paper)

Typeset in 11/13pt Palatino from author's disks by Text Processing Department,
John Wiley & Sons Ltd, Chichester
Printed and bound in Great Britain by
Biddles Ltd, Guildford and King's Lynn

To Fiona and Andrew, for all the quality time
this book took away!

CONTENTS

SERIES PREFACE

The aim of the Wiley Series in Clinical Psychology is to provide a comprehensive library of texts for the practising clinician. Between them, the books cover a range of topics of interest not only to psychologists, but also to a wide range of other professionals in mental health and community care settings. This volume, *Quality and Excellence in Human Services*, by Paul Dickens, is just such a book. The increased concern about quality of services compels us to examine thoroughly what we *mean* by quality; how it is best assessed; how might the pursuit of quality founder; how might it be rescued. Dickens goes back to the origins of the concept of quality in industry, and takes the reader through its development in service settings to its arrival as a concept in human services and health care settings. Such a comprehensive review, linking current quality issues with their original meanings, has not been done before. It will be an important book, the lessons from which apply across the spectrum of health and social care; in psychiatry; social work; clinical psychology; nursing; and professions allied to medicine, such as occupational therapy; speech and language therapy; and physiotherapy. For clinicians and their managers in these services, the issues of how to demonstrate quality is becoming paramount. Paul Dickens' book will be an excellent source of help in this endeavour.

J.M.G. Williams
Series Editor

CHAPTER 1   Introduction to quality and excellence

QUALITY IN HUMAN SERVICES

Times have changed. Once it was sufficient just to provide a service in the field of human services, regardless of how good that service was. Now, however, with greater concern about efficiency, effectiveness and quality in industry and public services, it is not enough just to *provide* a service; it must be demonstrated to be of sufficient quality to justify its continued existence. In one pertinent area of human services, namely mental health, of all the areas of human services, the provision of no service at all might be better than provision of a poor quality one, as the potential for human damage by an incompetent, unprofessional and generally low quality service is enormous.

There are a number of influences that have brought about this increased concern for quality. Firstly most public services in the Western world have come under increased financial restraint and, at the same time, increased public scrutiny. World recession has forced many countries into a re-examination of public spending priorities, with a consequent stress on cost effectiveness and efficiency. Services that provide poor value for money have found themselves either deprived of funds or put out to open tender with a view to improved competitiveness through "market forces". Competitive tendering in British public services is a good example of this in operation, and it also ensures greater managerial control over quality through the contracting process. Financial stringencies have also caused service providers to examine their priorities in terms of providing positive outcomes, so that services that cannot demonstrate effectiveness lose out to those that can. One of the advantages that the therapeutic professions have is their emphasis on the objective, scientific evaluation of outcome in treatment, so that clinical practice can usually be shown to be effective in both clinical and financial terms. As an example of this, the recent review of the profession of clinical psychology in the British National Health Service carried out by the Management Advisory Service included a valuable summary of the efficacy of psychological methods in mental health (Management Advisory Service, 1989).

A second influence causing increased concern for quality has been the major changes in values, organisational structure and operational methods that have occurred over the past five or so years in all areas of human services. Such changes include the introduction of care in the community and the move away from institutional care; the "deprofessionalisation" of many fields of human services with the consequent increase in self-help groups and a resulting redefinition of professional roles; greater use of holistic models of human functioning with less emphasis on pathological approaches and the introduction of new organisational structures often involving devolved management and financial control, contracted services and/or shifts in the location of services (for example from health service to social service control). Such changes often provide an opportunity for service purchasers and providers to evaluate the effectiveness and quality of the service provided, either for the purpose of investigating the effects of the change or as a means to accomplish the necessary cultural, philosophical or organisation changes themselves.

Thirdly, there has been the rise of consumer influence on service provision, and the greater importance attached to "customer satisfaction". Consumer groups have grown in numbers and influence in all fields of human services as a counterpart to their growth in commerce and industry. Advocacy groups are now commonplace in mental health services in many countries, and have an increasing influence on service models and methods. This can operate at an individual level, where an advocate or the person concerned may attempt to influence the services they receive, or at a group or class level where major changes in service provision are sought by groups or by people acting on their behalf. In the United States, for example, much of the change from institutional to community care for people with learning disability has been the result of humanitarian concern by lay people or by litigation against service providers who have failed to provide adequate services. Similarly, the importance of consumer opinion has been recognised in the planning and evaluation of services, echoing the increasing importance of customer satisfaction in commercial enterprises. Later in this book we will return to the issue of customer evaluation and satisfaction, but it is worth at this stage quoting the leading authors on this topic in the service industry field, Zeithaml, Parasuraman and Berry, who go so far as to say:

> The only criteria that count in evaluating service quality are defined by customers. Only customers judge quality; all other judgements are essentially irrelevant. Specifically service quality perceptions stem from how well a provider performs vis-à-vis customers' expectations about how the provider should perform. (Zeithaml, Parasuraman and Berry, 1990, p. 16)

The rise of consumer involvement in quality issues is in part a reflection of a fourth influence on the concern for quality, that of the general pre-eminence of quality as *the* topic for management and industry in the 1990s. In many ways quality has become something of a bandwagon, with fashionable topics such as "total quality management" dominating concerns, and with a large number of quality "gurus" selling their own ideas on what constitutes quality. Huczynski (1993) has analysed this phenomenon, and suggests that there are six major schools of management thought, the ideas of which are recycled by "gurus" who bring their own communicative skills to bear on the ideas, thereby popularising them. At the same time there have been serious attempts to improve the quality of industrial products and systems and of human services, including the development of quality accreditation schemes such as the International Standard for quality systems, ISO9000 (BS5750 in Britain). Such issues will be covered in more detail in Chapter 2 of this book.

Lastly, the concern for the quality of human services has been influenced by desires for professional identity which bring with them increased emphasis on training, both pre- and post-qualification, professional competence and professional legitimacy. The rise of the profession of clinical psychology in the British context is a good example of this, where the establishment of autonomy, identity and legitimacy has been hastened by the development of university-based professional training courses of increasing duration (for example the recent move from two- to three-year courses), which are the subject of peer scrutiny and accreditation (Committee on Training in Clinical Psychology, 1991) and by the establishment of the Register of Chartered Psychologists by the British Psychological Society in 1990. A good discussion of these and other trends regarding this therapeutic profession can be found in Pilgrim and Treacher (1992).

The Aim and Scope of this Book

Given this increased concern about the quality of human services, and the influences that have contributed to it, the aim of this book is to draw together work from a variety of sources to enable professionals from any discipline involved in the human services field to examine the quality of their service, and to improve it should this prove necessary. To do this it aims to review the issue of quality in service industries in general, and draw together this work with the literature on quality in various human services, something that has not been done before. Because this book has been written by a clinical psychologist, some of the source material comes from this area and concerns psychology as applied to health and social care. It has, however, general applicability to a range of other "therapeutic" professions, including psychiatry, social work, nursing and professions allied to medicine such as occupational therapy and speech and language therapy. It should also prove of interest to applied psychologists in specialty areas such as education and industry. As a result of this, a wide definition of terms is possible. "Quality" and "human services" are viewed on a general level, the former including concepts such as quality assurance, clinical audit, outcome evaluation and customer satisfaction, and the latter including many specialty areas such as mental health, learning disability, general and child health and old age. This broad brush approach might mean that detailed analysis of methods and topics is not possible. Where this is the case, sufficient reference material will be quoted for readers to pursue matters for themselves.

The Organisation of this Book

The first two chapters of this book will cover some of the essential background work on the topic of quality, firstly in its widest possible setting and in terms of the industrial background, and then secondly in service industries, which includes those undertakings that provide "human services", and that subsume most of the settings in which therapists work. The third chapter is particularly important in defining human services and discusses the further definition of quality within them, itself a difficult and detailed topic. It is therefore recommended that this is an "essential reading" section of the book for all those interested in using the ideas contained here.

These ideas lead naturally on to the fourth chapter, where we discuss the tools and techniques of quality control, assurance and management in general manufacturing and service industry settings. The next three chapters examine the same tools and techniques of quality in human services in general, and also focus on the specific techniques that have been developed in that context. Chapter 8 suggests some ways in which a systematic approach to quality assurance may be developed in human services and the therapeutic professions.

Lastly, in Chapter 9 we will consider the issue of quality of life, and how it affects judgements of service quality made both by professionals and by consumers, and discuss general issues raised in the course of the book concerning human service quality.

CHAPTER 2 The search for quality and excellence in industry

The current movement for high quality and excellent human services mirrors a similar position in manufacturing and service industries throughout the world. The increasingly competitive situation in public services means that, as in industry, quality equals customers equals money. This chapter will try first to define the terms we are using—quality and excellence—at their most general level, and then second to discuss quality against the background of industry and commerce, where many quality assurance ideas current in health and social care have their root. Lastly, we will look at the issue of quality and customer satisfaction in service industries, bearing in mind the quotation in the last chapter from Zeithaml, Parasuraman and Berry, on the crucial importance of customer expectation and satisfaction in the definition and description of quality services.

DEFINING QUALITY AND EXCELLENCE

Quality—you know what it is, yet you don't know what it is. But that's self-contradictory. But some things *are* better than others, that is, they have more quality. But when you try and say what quality is ... it all goes poof! What the hell is quality? What is it? (Pirsig, 1974, p. 239)

As with most areas, ideas and theories in psychology, agreement over definitions of quality in general is difficult and fraught with polemics, confusion and subjectivity. We all recognise quality in most areas of life, however. If asked to name a quality automobile, most people will say something like "Jaguar", "BMW" or "Rolls-Royce". Very few will say "Lada", "Skoda" or "Trabant". Similarly shops such as "Marks and Spencer" or "Niemann–Marcus" are generally held to be quality shops, selling quality merchandise, while "Poundstretchers" and "K-Mart" convey an altogether different image. If then asked to define why it is that certain names signify or conjure up an image of quality, matters become more complicated. The Lada and the BMW share certain common features—four wheels, engine, seats, etc.—and are suited to the purpose for which they were intended. Something is different between them that probably cannot be measured in terms of engineering tolerances, finish quality, etc. (although these are important differentiating factors). The name "BMW" carries an image or an aura of quality that is greater than the sum of these differences.

In the field of industrial production, the word quality has many applicable definitions. The following three definitions come from that area, and reflect differing views on the nature of quality:

Quality is:

> ... fitness for use. (Juran, 1988)

> ... conformance to requirements. (Crosby, 1979)

> ... the totality of features and characteristics of a product or service that bear on its ability to satisfy stated or implied needs. (British Standards Institute, 1992)

Later in this chapter we will look at the ideas and definitions of quality of, among others, Crosby and Juran, and the ISO9000 quality accreditation system will have a later section to itself. For now it is interesting that the relatively simple nature of the first two definitions—that fit with our car analogy—stress that primarily quality is about the ability of the product or service to "do the job", to meet specific quality criteria and specifications. As such they reflect a preoccupation of early quality work with manufacturing industries, particularly armaments and engineering, where quality is the ability of the product to meet the requirements of contractors and purchasers. The BSI definition is a wider interpretation of quality, and it includes ideas that will find an echo in our later discussions of quality in human services. It introduces the idea of need, and of meeting the needs of the person requiring the product or service, whether these are stated or implied. It also defines quality as the "totality of features and characteristics", the intangible essence that makes the service or product different from another.

The term "excellence" gained wide usage following a book by Peters and Waterman—*In Search of Excellence* (1982) that not only established the idea that the performance of "excellent" companies or organisations could be quantified, but also gave wider publicity to the management theories of its first author, Tom Peters, whose operational, no-nonsense approach to quality and excellence has become very popular in industry. Peters and Waterman set out to define excellence not only in terms of fiscal performance (long-term profitability), but also in organisational culture, management style and innovativeness. From a study of several defined companies and organisations in the United States they discerned those attributes that they consider embody the essence of excellent concerns, and provide a strategy for the development of quality and excellence in any setting. A similar study focusing on British companies and organisations was carried out by Goldsmith and Clutterbuck (1984), producing similar conclusions to those of their American counterparts.

The adequate definition of quality and excellence is a major problem, not least because there are so many conflicting, competing and confusing definitions. It is easiest to accomplish in the realm of manufacturing industry, where quality can be specified in terms of tolerances and performance criteria. In service industries, and particularly in the realm of human services, the problem of definition is acute, as we will explore here and in the next chapter. Smith (1986) has highlighted this issue, documenting the confusion caused to managers by the writings of so many "gurus" on the topic. He coins the term "Total Quality Paralysis" to describe this confusion, and suggests that so much time might be spent by managers trying to decide between the different definitions and interpretations, that they would not be able to take any action on developing quality as a result.

A Historical Perspective on Quality and Excellence

Although it is really only in the twentieth century that a "quality movement" has emerged, and specifically in the last twenty years, there has always been a concern for manufacturing industries to perform to standards, criteria or specifications of quality in their manufactured goods. In his recent historical review of quality management, Morrison (1990) points out that quality control is founded on measurement, which is an idea that can be traced back to primitive man, and early civilisations such as Babylon, Greece and Rome developed rapidly because they were able to standardise and specify according to measurable and measured criteria. Standards of weight and measure were laid down in medieval times. One of the foundations of quality control—interchangeable standard parts—owes its origin to the earliest printers, such as Caxton and Guttenberg, whose influence on the development of Western intellectual life, through the distribution of cheaply printed books, is profound.

In the history of quality assurance systems the armaments industries have a central place. Standards for the defence industries were first introduced in Britain in the reign of Charles I, and the mass production manufacturing processes that were developed as part of the Industrial Revolution during the eighteenth and nineteenth centuries were based on the idea of standardised interchangeable parts made to a controlled, standardised specification. The First World War acted as a stimulus in the further development of quality inspection systems, as shown by the establishment of the Technical Inspection Association, the forerunner of the Institute of Quality Assurance, in 1919. The influence of armament manufacturers on quality assurance and accreditation is still strong, with the British Ministry of Defence Procurement Executive playing a leading role in the development and introduction of standards, particularly BS5750/ISO9000.

A new impetus for quality assurance was provided during the early part of this century through the work of statisticians such as Pearson and Kendall, who developed the non-parametric methods of statistical analysis on which the principle and methods of statistical quality control processes depend. This concept is based on the theory of probability, and the use of sampling techniques and predictive statistics to analyse production data. A useful guide to these methods can be found in Oakland (1986), and a good discussion is in Shaw and Dale (1990). In 1935 the British Standards Institute adopted a set of practices and a system for accreditation based on statistical quality control, BS600, and the work of Deming (1982) and Taguchi (1986) in Japan after the Second World War not only furthered the statistical approach to quality assurance, but also laid the foundation for the Japanese manufacturing dominance in the late twentieth century.

Japan has an important place in any history of quality assurance. After the war, as already mentioned, Japanese industry was rebuilt and extended using all the available management methods from the United States, including statistical quality control. Added to this was the indigenous development of new manufacturing techniques that ensured the quality of the product. Quality circles were invented in Japan in the early 1960s, as an attempt to involve all workers in all aspects of the quality of the product. Total quality management methods are also a reflection of the Japanese approach to management, which in turn has its foundations in Japanese culture.

While things have not been as dynamic in Britain, one important contribution has been the recent development of quality assurance system standards by the British Standards Institute. BS5750, and its international counterpart ISO9000, has rapidly become the major international standard for the assessment and accreditation of such systems, and new industry has grown up in the area of establishing and inspecting them. The possession of BS5750/ISO9000 is a status symbol to manufacturing industry, and from 1992, to service industries as well.

Approaches to Quality in Industry

As we have seen, the major thrust in the early development of quality assurance systems came from manufacturing industry, and it is in this market sector that most of the theoretical writing on quality is to be found. The demand for standardised interchangeable manufactured parts of predictable performance led to the introduction of quality standards and specific manufacturing criteria, either by manufacturers or by purchasers, or both. The early focus of quality assurance schemes was therefore on inspection and monitoring of performance against predetermined standards.

Using statistical process control, batches of produced goods could be sampled, and the range of product variability calculated. If this range was found to be greater than the specified tolerance, then the process could be adjusted to bring the quality of the final product in line with the specification. The author recently visited a chocolate factory and observed this type of quality control in action. A 10% sample of all chocolate bars was taken off the production line to a separate table where the external appearance was assessed, and the weight measured. If either of these variables, or any others measured, fell outside a predetermined range, then the whole production batch was scrapped and recycled. One implication of this type of approach is that it is a post-hoc analysis of quality. It soon became apparent, particularly to the Japanese, that the key to improved quality was to focus on developing the manufacturing process itself, so that quality was built in at the earliest possible stage. This found expression in the "Right First Time" philosophy espoused by, among others, Crosby (1979), and was justified on the grounds of better financial performance. (*Quality is Free* is the title of Crosby's seminal work.)

The logical next step was to apply the same specification process that governed the manufacturing process to the quality assurance system itself, producing the type of system represented by ISO9000, where the emphasis is on developing an inspection and control system that in itself meets specified standards. The implication is that such a system would have a direct bearing on the quality of the manufactured product, as it ensures quality throughout the process, and emphasises prevention rather than cure. Another vital element in this is the role of "third party agencies" who accredit the systems. These bodies might be external agencies of accreditation, such as the BSI, or powerful purchasers. It is well known, for example, that Marks and Spencer expect the highest standards of production from their suppliers and have strict quality control standards that are regularly reviewed. Suppliers that do not meet the standards (which also can cover staff working conditions and management competence) soon find themselves without a lucrative and high-status contract. Losing a Marks and Spencer contract is worse than never having had one in the first place.

The final logical shift is from quality assurance schemes to an approach that stresses quality as the responsibility of all staff, and as pervading all aspects of the company's work. This includes not just the manufacturing process, but also the management, support, marketing and personnel functions. At this level the concern for quality merges with wider issues such as management style and strategy, leadership and the organisational culture. Peters and Waterman (1982) consider these variables to be of greater predictive value of quality performance and product than mere product sampling. Developing this total approach requires a much more "psychological" approach to the issue, stressing team building and organisational dynamics.

Dale, Lascelles and Plunkett (1990) outline a four-level model of the evolution of quality management, that is similar to the one outlined above:

- *Level One: Inspection*—one or more characteristics of a product are inspected, measured or tested and compared with specified requirements to assess its conformity. This is done mainly by staff employed to carry out this task, and it does not involve the production workers. Non-conforming parts are scrapped or returned for reworking.

- *Level Two: Quality Control*—the same emphasis on inspection but involving the production workers and feedback systems to the production line so that the production process can be modified to produce conforming goods.

- *Level Three: Quality Assurance*—systematic and planned actions to produce conforming articles, internal audit and external evaluation to ensure continued quality. Systems of quality assurance would be specified and followed, and their implementation monitored.

- *Level Four: Total Quality Management*—the application of quality management procedures to all aspects of the business, including policy setting, strategy, organisational structure and culture.

Approaches to Quality—the Message of the Quality "Gurus"

Earlier in this chapter we mentioned the conceptual confusion— "Total Quality Paralysis"—that has been caused by so many conflicting definitions and ideas on quality in industry. In this field there are several recognised "gurus", whose writings and achievements have had a major influence on industrial processes and management structures and styles in many countries. It is worth examining the basic tenets of the principal people in this field, whose names have already been mentioned: Crosby, Deming, Juran and Taguchi. No doubt other names could be included, but it is generally accepted that these four are the most influential writers on the subject of quality and the development of quality management (Fine, 1985).

Philip Crosby

Crosby's famous dictum—"quality is free!"—has already been quoted, and it illustrates his concern with the financial effects of quality improvement. His definition of quality, mentioned above, stresses the fact that quality is based primarily on conformity to a set of specified standards. In his most seminal work (1979), he outlined five basic principles of quality management:

1. Quality means conformance not elegance.
2. There is no such thing as a quality problem, but there may be an engineering or a marketing problem.
3. It is always cheaper to do the job right first time.
4. The only useful performance indicator is the cost of quality.
5. The only performance standard is zero defects.

From these principles he devised a measurement tool of quality achievement in a company, the quality management maturity grid, stressing a stepwise approach to quality that he then outlines in detail with a fourteen-step quality improvement programme. Central to his work is the twofold idea that quality is merely conformity, and that conformity means reduced costs and increased profit. He stresses the importance of quality managers in a company, and in many ways supports traditional hierarchical management structures, with less emphasis on the involvement of shopfloor workers than other writers. Simple in concept, Crosby's approach can be criticised for being over-simplistic concerning implementation, neglecting the idea of excellence and supporting traditional working practices that might not in themselves be sufficient to deliver quality in the present economic and trading climate.

W. Edwards Deming

Deming has a reputation as the man who transformed Japanese industry after the Second World War. While this is only partly true, his major writings (1982) show the extent to which his own work has been influenced by Japanese business practices and management styles. In contrast to Crosby, he is less concerned with the economic aspects of quality, but more with the effects of quality on productivity and marketing. Deming's definition of quality stresses three areas that are crucial for the overall quality of a product: quality of design; quality of conformance; quality of the sales and service functions. He suggests that the major economic factor is the cost of selling defective products to customers. Deming also stresses the importance of statistical quality control, with the emphasis on using these techniques to reduce variation in product conformance to specification. He also comes close to the total quality management school by stressing the importance of involving all employees in the quality improvement process, and even suggests that all employees should receive training in statistical quality techniques. The Japanese influence is strong here, with the emphasis Deming places on training at all levels and the need for management to be involved with, and actively implement, the message of quality.

Joseph Juran

Closer to Crosby in his approach than to Deming, Juran stresses the need for companies to reduce the cost of quality. He also adopts a similarly restrictive definition of quality, as we have already seen above. This definition—"fitness for use"—is split into four areas, rather like Deming's: quality of design; quality of conformance; quality of service; availability. Juran's approach also stresses the strategic aspects of quality management systems, and he outlines three areas that need to be addressed: sporadic problems, that need to be tackled by control mechanisms to prevent the occurrence of defects; chronic problems, that can be managed by encouraging good practice; and annual quality improvement, which must be a strategic issue tackled by top management. Again, rather like Crosby, Juran stresses the traditional hierarchical model of management, and places importance on quality professionals and middle managers as the main arbiters of quality improvement, with less responsibility devolving to shopfloor workers.

Genichi Taguchi

Taguchi is the major name in the field of statistical process control, and has given his name to the so-called "Taguchi methods" of experimental and statistical quality analysis. A good discussion of the application of Taguchi's ideas is to be found in Disney and Bendall (1990). There are two principal ideas in Taguchi's work: "the loss function" and "off-line quality control". In the former he defines quality in terms of the loss suffered by a product when it does not reach an adequate level of quality. This loss may be expressed as customer dissatisfaction, costs of replacement or repair, loss of market image, and loss of market share. In keeping with his highly statistical approach, Taguchi considers that a product causes this loss not only when it does not meet specification, but also when it deviates from a target value. Quality improvement is therefore to be achieved by measuring and minimising variance in production. The second principle, "off-line quality control", stresses the vital importance of reducing product variability in the design process. He advocates the use of experimental techniques to vary systematically the design characteristics of a product in order to measure the effect of this on production. Taguchi represents a bridge between the Crosby–Juran style of quality system management and that of Deming and the statisticians of statistic process control. His influence on Japanese, and Western, manufacturing industry has been profound.

QUALITY IN SERVICE INDUSTRIES

The work of the so-called "gurus" described above, and indeed the main thrust of the approaches to quality so far discussed, has been towards the problem of improving the quality of manufactured goods. In this area, quality is tangible, and can be defined, observed and measured in terms of the characteristics and specifications of the required product. In the realm of service industries, however, things are much less easily defined, and quality becomes more of the abstract concept that was alluded to at the start of this chapter. The central focus can be seen to be the attitude of the service towards, and the interaction process with, the customer—"customer care" as it is often called. Before looking at the issue of quality in service industries, we must first set out some of the characteristics of such industries that affect the establishment of a quality service product. This is an important area of discussion, as most therapeutic and psychological practices are service industries of a specific kind: "human services".

Defining a Service Industry

However we define a service industry, it is evident that to a greater or lesser extent all organisations involve some degree of service. Large manufacturing companies, such as an automobile company like Rover or BMW, also must provide service, both internally (such as human resources, finance and marketing) to other branches of the company that are more closely involved in the production side, and externally, to agents and, most importantly, customers (such as after-sales service). Indeed, as the quality of the produced goods improves, and the competitive advantage gained from increased quality becomes less (as other competing manufacturers also develop better quality products), then the attention of the organisation must be directed to the service components, where the competitive edge might be restored by offering better quality service to customers. As we have already seen, the overwhelming trend in quality assurance has been towards the production of tangible goods, and the improvement of those goods through the improvement of the manufacturing, inspection and management control processes. The trend in economic life over recent years, particularly in most Western countries, has been away from manufacturing industry and toward services. In the United Kingdom in 1950 there were approximately 8 520 000 workers employed in manufacturing against 3 573 000 employed in services. By 1975 the position had reversed, so that in 1983 there were 5 641 000 workers employed in manufacturing and 9 222 000 employed in services.

There has been a steady increase in the amount written on the subject of quality in service industries that mirrors the rise in market position mentioned above. The seminal works in the field are by Rosander (1990), the collection of papers edited by Brian Moores (1986) and the work of Zeithaml, Parasuraman and Berry (1988, 1990). A Scandinavian influence is strong in this area, which is summarised in the book edited by Brown, Gummesson, Edvardsson and Gustavsson (1991), and appears in the work of Gronroos (1988) and Lehtinen and Lehtinen (1991). A third force is the work of the Japanese writer Kano, and his colleagues (Kano, Seraku, Takahashi and Tsuji, 1984).

Most authors on the topic of service industries stress that services are different in three fundamental ways from manufacturing industries in terms of how they are produced, consumed and evaluated.

Firstly, services are *intangible*. They cannot be touched, tasted or constructed. They represent experiences, processes and performances, and as a result, the use of precise manufacturing and conformance specifications is impossible. There are tangible aspects to services, as we shall see later, but the service itself is still intangible, and similarly the service may lead to tangible results that may be observed and measured, such as a change in client behaviour because of service delivery. Because of this intangibility, the criteria that may be used to evaluate and assess the quality of the service will be complex, and more difficult to measure than in manufacturing industry.

Secondly, services are *heterogeneous*. Their performance differs from provider to provider, even within the same service sector, or indeed within the same service organisation. To standardise a service would be to standardise interactions that occur in the context of human interaction processes, skills and fallibilities. Uniformity in specification and conformity to standard, as in manufacturing industry, is not possible, as the service delivery situation is open to the influence of far more variables, most of which are difficult to control in any meaningful and monitorable way.

Thirdly, in services, *production and consumption of the service are inseparable*. Because the essence of service delivery is in the interaction between customer and service, the quality of the product of the service is the quality that is directly consumed by the customer. In manufacturing industry there is a buffer between production—say in a factory—and the consumption of the product—usually following purchase through an intervening body, the sales force. The customer is therefore directly involved with, and indeed is a prerequisite for, service delivery. Without a customer, the service does not exist, because the service is the process of interaction with that customer. Similarly, typically a service professional has only one opportunity to provide the service in a quality way, and the service product is instantly perishable.

The vital part of every service industry is to be found in the inter-action between the service provider and the service customer. Solomon and colleagues (Solomon, Suprenant, Czepiel and Gutman, 1985, and Czepiel, Solomon and Suprenant, 1985), suggest that this service encounter is a dyadic interaction between service provider and service customer, which has effects on the customers in terms of the overall quality experienced by them and therefore on their perceptions of the quality of the interaction, and on the service provider, by virtue of the effect of the encounter on motivation, job satisfaction and rewards. This encounter has been termed by Solomon et al. as "the moment of truth", which is defined by them as critical incidents in which customers come into contact with the organisation and form their impressions of quality and service.

The recent extension of the BS5750/ISO9000 quality standard to service industries has provided a useful working definition of a service industry, the one to which the standard might apply. This document defines a service as:

> The results generated by activities at the interface between the supplier and the customer and by supplier internal activities, to meet customer needs.
>
> 1. The supplier or customer may be represented at the interface by personnel or equipment.
> 2. Customer activities at the interface may be essential to the delivery of a service.
> 3. Delivery or use of tangible goods may form part of the service.
> 4. A service may be linked with the manufacture and supply of a tangible product. (ISO9004-2, 1991, p. 2)

The service delivery process may be highly mechanised, such as a directly dialled telephone call, or highly personalised, such as medical or psychological services. Similarly, the degree of involvement with a product might vary along a continuum, with high product involvement at one end (services such as car repair and maintenance) and low product involvement at the other (services such as psychotherapy and counselling).

The BSI document also lists the types of service industry to which the standard might apply, a list that contains such diverse examples as waste management, opticians, banking, architects, photographers and schools.

Specifying Quality in Service Industries

The three factors described above make the specification of a quality service exceptionally difficult. Barbara Lewis, in a recent review of quality in service industries (1989), points out that there are no clear-cut definitions of service quality, and no definitive techniques for its measurement. As a result the development and evaluation of quality service systems is extremely variable throughout service industries.

In a manufacturing context, as we have seen, the quality of the product can be made the subject of tolerance and production criteria that can be inspected, measured and subjected to the rigorous statistical analysis of techniques such as statistical process control. In many instances these specifications are set by the customer, the purchaser, who determines the requisite standard of quality expected in the supplied goods. A similar situation holds in service industries, where the customer sets the specifications, not in terms of tolerance and standards, but in terms of expectancies. It is very difficult for consumers of services, because of the variables mentioned above, to judge or measure how well a service is being performed in absolute terms, and they may use not just outcome criteria (how well the haircut looked) but also process criteria (how friendly the hair stylist was, how responsive to conversation, etc.). In this respect consumers of services will have expectations of how a service should be provided, based on previous experience, advertising, social interaction and peer report. The main message of Zeithaml, Parasuraman and Berry is that service quality is the degree to which customers' satisfaction with a service meets the expectancies they had about that service before using it. In arriving at this conclusion they distinguish between objective quality, which is mechanistic and is the quality of the production line, and perceived quality that is humanistic and:

> is the consumer's judgement about an entity's overall excellence and superiority. (Parasuraman, Zeithaml and Berry, 1988)

Given these factors Zeithaml and her colleagues (Parasuraman, Zeithaml and Berry, 1985) attempted to do two tasks: firstly to define the dimensions along which services differ on perceived quality; and secondly to devise a measurement tool that could objectively assess the expectancies and satisfaction of service users.

The Dimensions of Service Quality and Customer Satisfaction

The two issues outlined above started by using a technique from the field of marketing. Twelve "focus groups" covering four service industry sectors—retail banking, credit cards, securities broking and product repair and maintenance—were set up. The results from these discussion groups led to several conclusions:

1. Service quality as perceived by customers can be defined as the extent of discrepancy between customers' expectations or desires and their perceptions.

2. Several key factors shape customer expectations:

    (a) Word of mouth communications.

    (b) Personal needs of customers.

    (c) Extent of past experience in using a service.

    (d) External communications from the service providers.

    (e) Price of the service.

3. It is possible to define ten dimensions along which customers' expectations of service varied. These are outlined, together with examples, in Table 1.

Using these ten dimensions, Parasuraman, Zeithaml and Berry (1988) developed an assessment tool—SERVQUAL—that could be

Table 1   The ten dimensions of service quality.

Dimension	Definition	Example
Tangibles	Appearance of physical facilities, equipment, staff and communication materials	Does the service have pleasant offices?
Reliability	Ability to perform the promised service dependably and accurately	Is the contracted service always delivered?
Responsiveness	Willingness to help clients and provide prompt service	Do service staff always try and help you?
Competence	Possession of the required skills to perform the service	Are the staff good at their job?
Courtesy	Politeness, respect, consideration and friendliness of staff	Do staff treat you with respect?
Credibility	Trustworthiness, believability and honesty of staff	Do you trust the staff?
Security	Freedom from danger, risk or doubt	Do you feel safe using the service?
Access	Approachability and ease of contact	Is the service easy to get to?
Communication	Keeping clients informed in language they can understand, and listening to them	Do staff inform you about your treatment?
Understanding the client	Making efforts to know the clients and their needs	Do you think staff know your personal needs?

Adapted from Zeithaml, Parasuraman and Berry (1990)

used to measure both customer expectations and satisfaction in specific service industries and businesses. Preliminary work and item analysis of this questionnaire were subjected to factor analysis that produced five factors from the original ten dimensions in Table 1. These were:

- *Tangibles*—appearance of physical facilities, equipment, personnel and communication materials.

- *Reliability*—ability to perform the promised service dependably and accurately.

- *Responsiveness*—willingness to help customers and provide prompt service.

- *Assurance*—from the original dimensions of Competence, Courtesy, Credibility and Security. Knowledge and courtesy of employees and their ability to convey trust and confidence.

- *Empathy*—from the original dimensions of Access, Communication and Understanding the Customer. Caring and individualised attention the firm provides its customers.

Further research has shown that service companies vary in the relative importance attached to each of the above dimensions, with reliability being a critical dimension, despite the type of industry, and tangibles being of least importance. Carman (1990) addressed several issues concerning SERVQUAL, including the number and generic nature of the dimensions. He found, using information on a variety of service industries, that only Responsiveness, Tangibles and Security were common over all settings, while there was variation over settings in the factor structure of the other two dimensions. This was not large enough to invalidate the factors, but just enough to encourage caution in the use of the scale.

Carman also addressed an issue that is central to the measurement of quality in service industries (and particularly in health care), that of multiple service functions. In most service settings, the interaction between the customer and the service takes place on many occasions, and might even be a cluster of interactions with several service personnel. (Think about the process of being seen in a hospital casualty department, which might involve interaction and a "product" from many staff.) Carman used a hospital as one of his sources of information, and found a difference from all the other service industries in the clustering of dimensions, whilst Schlegelmilch, Carman and Moore (1992) have also extended the use of SERVQUAL to medical settings. We will discuss this further in a later chapter on consumer views on service quality.

In addition Carman discusses the question of the interaction between expectations and perceptions. He suggests that expectations are relatively consistent and durable dimensions, which may not vary greatly for each service industry. On the other hand perceptions are more transient, and subject to greater degrees of variability. In order to measure the quality of service provided, it is necessary to measure customers' expectations, but this might be done in a general way, and not at every administration of SERVQUAL.

Furthermore, the question of the relative importance of customer expectancies needs to be considered. As Carman suggests, the competence of a surgeon is more important than the art on the hospital wall. He attempts to define this by a linear equation, where overall quality (Q) is an attitude, a multidimensional construct composed of differences between perceptions (P) and expectations (E):

$$Q = \Sigma I_i (P_i - E_i)$$

where: I is the importance of service attribute i.

This equation shows that all three variables, importance, perception and expectations, are relevant and crucial factors in the measurement of service quality, and Carman's contribution is to stress the vital role of the importance dimension when considering customer satisfaction.

There have been a number of challenges to Parasuraman, Zeithaml and Berry's conclusions. Cronin and Taylor (1992) criticise them on several grounds. Firstly, they suggest that there is very little evidence to support the thesis that the expectations–performance gap is the basis for measuring service quality, pointing out that there is a substantial body of literature to support the superiority of simple performance measures of service quality. To this end they test and report a version of SERVQUAL—called SERVPERF—that is a pure performance measure. Secondly, they suggest that there has been little research on the effect of service quality, customer satisfaction and purchasing intentions, so that there is little evidence of the causal links between all three. Lastly, they question the conclusion that service quality can be equated with customer satisfaction, suggesting that perceived service quality is a form of attitude, a long-running overall evaluation, while satisfaction is a transaction-specific measure. They stress the importance of experience-based, rather than expectation-based, norms for comparing against performance in measuring service quality. More importantly, they distinguish service quality and customer satisfaction as two distinct constructs, related in that satisfaction mediates the effect of prior perceptions of service quality to allow customers to formulate a revised perception following interaction with the service. In this way service quality is an antecedent of customer satisfaction. Distinguishing between these two constructs, Cronin and Taylor's research provides some evidence for the causal link between customer satisfaction and purchasing intentions, which they show to be stronger than the link between service quality and purchasing intentions.

Other Approaches to Defining Service Quality

By way of contrast to the work of Zeithaml, Parasuraman and Berry, the Scandinavian approach referred to earlier has a simpler framework at its heart. Gronroos (1988) outlined three dimensions of service quality:

1. The *technical quality* of the outcome of the service encounter, that represents the tangible product of the service.

2. The *functional quality* of the process itself, which is the manner in which the service is provided through the medium of the service encounter.

3. The *corporate image* dimension which is a global view of the company as perceived by the customer, built from the first two dimensions and established over time.

Gronroos also discusses the concept of a "service offering". This is the product of the service, and is composed of two items: a basic service package, which is the core service being delivered; and an augmented service offering, that represents the totality of the interaction between service and customer.

A similar definition of quality is developed by Lehtinen and Lehtinen (1991), who like Gronroos, distinguish three dimensions of service quality that are related to the service product:

1. *Physical quality*, which consists of the physical elements of the service. These fall into two categories, *physical support*, that includes the environment and service tools or instruments that enable the production of the service, and *physical product*, that may be minimal in those services that are more intangible.

2. *Interactive quality*, which is the quality of the interaction between the customer and the service provider at the "moment of truth".

3. *Corporate quality*, which is developed during a history of contact between service provider and customer, and is to do with the symbolic way in which customers see the service provider's corporate entity, image and profile. It is stable over time, and based on a number of interactions and perceptions of the first two dimensions.

To this Lehtinen and Lehtinen add two further dimensions that concern the customer's perception of the service:

1. *Process quality*, which is a customer's qualitative evaluation of their participation in the service process, that may vary on a scale of intensity from light to heavy, and consists of subjective judgements and experiences.

2. *Output quality*, which is the customer's evaluation of the outcome of the service interaction process. It may also be judged by "third persons", who can also see the outcome by way of its effect on the customer or by their word of mouth transmission of the product.

Lastly, the Japanese work of Kano and his colleagues should be mentioned. In their 1984 paper they propose a two-way model of service quality, based on two aspects: an objective aspect involving the presence or absence of a quality attribute (i.e. its fulfilment or unfulfilment) and a subjective aspect involving the user's resulting sense of satisfaction or dissatisfaction. Using a structured questionnaire, Kano outlines a number of categories of the user's perception of quality. These are:

1. *Attractive quality element*, an attribute whose presence gives satisfaction but whose absence is accepted without causing dissatisfaction.

2. *One-dimensional quality element*, an attribute whose presence gives satisfaction and whose absence causes dissatisfaction.

3. *Must-be quality element*, an attribute whose presence is accepted without creating satisfaction, but whose absence causes dissatisfaction.

4. *Indifferent quality element,* an attribute whose presence or absence give neither satisfaction nor dissatisfaction.

5. *Reverse quality element,* an attribute whose presence causes dissatisfaction and whose absence gives satisfaction.

Schvaneveldt, Enkawa and Miyakawa (1991) have used these categorisations to rate a number of quality dimensions drawn from a factor analytic study of consumer evaluations of a range of service industries. The factors used were:

1. *Performance,* which is the core function of a service and its level of achievement. It is results-orientated.

2. *Assurance,* which is the accuracy and responsiveness in providing the core service function, and the sense of assurance or trust that evolves as a result. Assurance is process-orientated, and emphasises the manner in which the service is delivered.

3. *Completeness,* which means the availability and variety of peripheral services and amenities beyond the core service function.

4. *Ease of use,* which is the accessibility, simplicity and facility of use of the service.

5. *Emotion/environment,* which is the sense of well-being or satisfaction felt by the customer beyond the fulfilment of the core service function, and corresponding to employee courtesy, atmosphere and physical environment.

Combining these aspects, Schvaneveldt, Enkawa and Miyakawa suggest that some aspects of service quality are essential ("must-be"), mainly assurance, whilst others, such as ease of use, performance and emotion/environment are one dimensional. Completeness is indifferent. The authors also examine longer term changes in these dimensions and attributes as a result of service experience.

Service Quality

No matter how service quality is defined and measured, it is apparent that there are a number of consistent findings from research. The attributes of service quality derive from customers' expectancies and experiences and the satisfaction, or dissatisfaction, that those experiences provide. The experiences themselves are relatively intangible, so that measuring and controlling them in a meaningful way is difficult if not impossible, and they also vary in relative importance across situations and individuals. The relationship between these dimensions and the actual choice of a service is influenced more by customer satisfaction, a relatively transient and short-term factor, than by general perceptions of service quality, which are more durable and long-term. Davidow and Uttal (1989), in a seminal text on customer service in service industries, state:

> Since most attributes of service quality are so closely linked to customers' experiences you can't do a final inspection for service quality in the absence of customers. Thus setting up service standards and monitoring variations in service production, just as companies monitor variations from a set of technical standards when manufacturing a product, is a myopic way to control service quality ... To complicate matters further, customers weigh the attributes of service quality differently according to their expectations ... Since service quality consists of a bundle of experience qualities weighted by customer expectations, classical, product-oriented quality control programs are impotent. (Davidow and Uttal, 1989, pp. 194–195)

It is obvious that a realistic assessment of service industry quality, and any practical, effective way of improving that quality, will have to consider these factors. Besides product-orientated measures, which might account for the more tangible aspects of services in some sectors, there will need to be consideration of process-orientated variables, which will cover the interactional aspects of service provision. Lastly, the dimensions of customer expectancies and satisfaction need to be considered, given their vital importance in determining service quality.

CONCLUSIONS

In this chapter we have considered the issue of quality from the point of view of industry in general, and finally from that of service industries. We have reviewed the definitions of quality that have guided both the evaluation of quality and the development of quality management and assurance programmes in manufacturing industries, and have looked at the historical factors that have led to such developments as ISO9000. In considering the views of the so-called quality "gurus", the roots of confusion and complexity in quality development can be seen. Lastly, the difficulties of defining, monitoring and developing quality in service industries have been highlighted.

All of the above issues are relevant when we begin to examine quality in the field of human services, which in themselves are just a particular section of the service industry field, and are therefore also subject to all the factors described in detail above. In addition there are specific factors introduced by the nature of human services, as we shall see in the next chapter, that make quality an even more complicated issue. The lasting message of the present chapter however—the crucial importance of customer expectations, experiences and satisfaction in the definition, development and measurement of the quality of service industries—will remain in our forthcoming discussions.

CHAPTER 3   Quality and excellence in human services

ISSUES IN HUMAN SERVICES

As we saw in the last chapter, service industries are complex, and the definition, measurement and establishment of quality within them reflect this. In this chapter we will look at the issue of quality and excellence in that subsection of the service industry sector considered as "human services", and examine some of the ways in which quality and excellence have been conceptualised and measured in many diverse service situations. From the very general discussions of the earlier part of the last chapter we focused more narrowly in the latter part on service industries, and now we focus more narrowly again on the particular sector—health and disability care in its widest form—that is the concern of most readers of this book. Despite this narrowing of focus, the lessons from the more general work on quality remain relevant, and will be applied.

Defining Human Services

In the last chapter we saw that service industries differ from manufacturing industries in three distinct ways: their products are largely intangible; they are heterogeneous; and production and consumption are inseparable. Our review of the research work has shown that the judgement of service quality is mainly concerned with the perceptions, attitudes and expectancies of its customers, for whom the service *is* the product, as opposed to manufacturing industry, where the judgement of quality is mainly in terms of the quality—or "fitness for use"—of the product itself. As most service industries deliver their product through the interaction between service personnel and customers (at least in most instances—a bank cash dispenser may be one of the alternative ways), then most service industries could lay claim to be "human services". For the purpose of this discussion, and throughout the book, however, we will define human services in a more specific way.

Human services are those service industries that are mainly concerned with supplying their product—services for people—in the areas of social, health and educational care. This definition includes all those who attempt the improvement, amelioration or clarification of human problems, and provide welfare or care services. There are several features that will further define this group of industries, and also form a background against which the consideration of quality and excellence must be made.

The Influence of Values

Human services usually operate on a more or less explicit values base, which is usually rooted in humanitarian concern. This may be concern for the physical or mental suffering of people who use the service (or who may be potential users) or concern for their welfare and development through care, treatment or education. Many value systems in human services have long historical traditions, for example the alleviation of human suffering as the fundamental value in medicine, or may be recent adoptions, such as the widespread acceptance of the principles of normalisation or social role valorisation in learning disability services. Sometimes these values may be expressed as a form of corporate "mission" or philosophy statement or, by way of contrast, they might exist as an implicit culture or operational style. This might not be articulated or even exist at a conscious level, as Wolfensberger (1987) suggests. The same author has traced the change in values in human services over time, and shown how social and political movements and professional influences have shifted early enlightened value systems into rigid and conformist philosophies. Later we will look at the importance of explicit values in the establishment of quality services.

Sources of Finance

Human services are, in most Western countries, provided or financed mainly, directly or indirectly by government, charitable or voluntary bodies. The proportion of this type of funding versus private funding might vary. In most areas—health care, education and social welfare—government either supplies the service through statutory agencies, or is responsible for its funding through money paid to non-statutory or even commercial providers. This money might be in the form of block grants, or on a "per case" basis. Exceptions to this might be insurance-funded private health care, private residential care for elderly people or independent private schools, but the proportion of this in relation to government-funded care or education is small.

Another feature of this aspect is that often the customer is not in a direct cash-paying relationship with the service. In most conventional service industries, the customer (whoever that might be, an individual or an organisation) has a cash relationship with the service provider, which may vary on a continuum of directness. In human services, however, often no money changes hands between the two parties, at any level of directness. The patient visiting the family medic does not pay anything directly to the physician for his or her services. The physician is paid by an authority (perhaps a family or primary health service agency) or by an agency (such as an insurance company) that acts as a broker or proxy for the patient. The only financial contribution is made through the remote method of taxation, and as such is divorced and disassociated from the point of service delivery. This is a crucial feature when considering the customer satisfaction levels of human services, as it negates the idea of open competition and the market force of value for money, except at the most general of levels.

The Heterogeneity of Human Services

Most human services involve a heterogeneous, multiprofessional service input, which in many cases is one of the major service features—for example a community mental health team. Although one or more professions may predominate in terms of the service provided—for example physicians and nurses in acute hospitals—others are an essential part of the service package, and the customers may well be more influenced by their interactions with these others than by those with the main service providers. The crucial "moment of truth", for example in a therapy clinic, might not be initially with a therapist, but with a receptionist. Human services also tend to employ a wide range of staff across widely differing levels of educational and vocational training and competence. A hospital has at one level porters and cleaners and at another surgeons and anaesthetists. Unfortunately one result of this is that many human services are dominated by interprofessional power struggles, which can detract from the quality of service provided. Another result is that the quality of the service is often a factor of professional competence, which is difficult for the average consumer to judge, and may be bound up in professional mystique and jargon to make this judgement more difficult. It also has implications for the development of quality services, and suggests that the total quality approach, where all levels and disciplines of staff are involved in quality actions, is desirable.

The Issue of Choice

Another feature of many human services is that the clients have not personally directly chosen to use that service. In other service industries, choice operates at an individual level. When booking a hotel in a holiday resort, an individual has an enormous choice that can be exercised, bearing in mind constraints such as price, position, services and availability. In human services, there often is no option but to use the few service providers available. In some countries or areas this might be a single agency or person. Take it or leave it! In the past this has caused human service to be complacent concerning quality, but recent government initiatives have attempted to introduce a market for services, with the introduction of an element of choice, even if from limited alternatives. Parental choice of school within the state sector (this was always the case in the private sector) is well established. In other areas, particularly the so-called "Cinderella services" such as residential care for elderly people or people with learning disabilities, choice is not an issue, as there is a general dearth of services to any adequate level.

A related issue is the fact that in the selection of many types of human service, the choice is not made by the consumer, but by another person acting on their behalf. Indeed the customer may not know what service it is they require, or even that they require it in the first place. The patient visiting the GP is referred to a hospital of the GP's choice, or to a therapist of the GP's choice. The patient has little or no knowledge of the service that may be offered by the consultant or hospital to which they have been referred, or even that they needed treatment for the condition in the first place. Social workers find care placements for people with learning disabilities, and negotiate on their behalf. The profoundly handicapped person with whom the social worker is dealing has no conception or knowledge of the type of residential care that will be made available. This calls into question the issue of whom the client is in human services. The service consumer may not be the service client, given what has already been said about the method of payment for human services. Furthermore, there may be many service clients, if it is accepted that all who use the service, at whatever level of directness, are defined as clients. Both the doctor and the patient are clients of the hospital at the same time, as are the social worker and the person with learning disability. What may differ is the intensity of the customer–service relationship, to use the ideas of Lehtinen and Lehtinen, with the doctor's intensity of contact being light, and the patient's heavy. Once again this has important implications for the definition and development of quality. It may be that the judgement of the quality of the service will be very different between the person experiencing the service and the person who selected, procured or financed the service for them.

Human Services as Service Industries

Given these vital factors, it is obvious that at the very least, human services are a very special type of service industry, with major differences from other more conventional types. At one extreme they may be seen as placed at the "high process–low product" end of a continuum of services, and therefore open to the same variables in the definition of quality as other similar service industries. Vuori (1982) suggests that an even more mechanistic view may be taken of human service quality, particularly health care. He develops the idea that health care is a form of production, and as such is open to the use of the same processes of quality control and assurance as other industries. The raw material consists of patients, who trigger a production process of care on entry into the system. Some of these processes follow a production line: history taking, diagnosis, treatment, rehabilitation and follow-up. The production process consists of the tasks and duties carried out by the various health care personnel involved. A final product is the outcome: a healthy or treated patient. Vouri suggests that even highly complex and specialised professional processes can be subjected to quality control procedures, if the focus shifts from product to process. For quality control procedures to be effective, however, they must be applied at every stage, to cover all aspects of the health care process.

Others take a different view, and stress the uniqueness of human services, because of their main concern with interpersonal relationships and the caring and therapeutic process. Dowson (1991), for example, has argued the inappropriateness of conventional organisational and management models and cultures in the field of services for people with learning disability, because of their inability to cope with the varied and flexible demands of the consumers. He suggests a move away from bureaucratic, management-dominated structures to looser communities and networks of involved people. The models of quality used in industry become irrelevant, as the only type of quality that is important is the quality of relationships and life satisfaction, which is a personal, subjective concept. Similarly, Williamson (1991) has pointed out a number of ways in which industrial and health care quality assurance differ. Firstly, he suggests that health care is not so completely outcome-orientated as a manufacturing process, where the total aim of the procedure is to produce an expected outcome—the finished product. In health care, the outcome expected will differ with the age, fitness and general health of the patient. Therefore the emphasis of medicine is on the input, rather than the outcome. The patient—the raw material of Vuori—is also not standard, and the process adopted to produce an outcome will therefore differ in each case, making specification difficult. The process itself may also differ, and have multiple or single components, which may in themselves be distorted by side effects which require attention. Williamson states secondly that quality control procedures are not relevant to health care, as sampling and destructive testing are not possible in the same way as they are on a production line. Thirdly, he considers that much health care is judgemental, particularly where it concerns professional decisions. Lastly, he points out that the raw material of health care is not inert, as it would be in some manufacturing process, but is very actively involved in treatment and has a definite view on the processes and expected outcomes. Williamson, however, can be criticised because his analogies are with manufacturing industries and not with service industries. As we have seen in the last chapter, these are different in many ways, and the applicability of the concepts derived from research on service industries to human services is far clearer.

Both these opposing viewpoints agree, however, on the fact that human services are service industries with a high "intangibles" component, in which the interaction processes between consumer and provider are the crucial element in the determination of the quality of service and of the assessment of the service quality by customer and provider alike. These interaction processes may involve extremely subtle judgements being made by the consumer, with cues from the interpersonal skills of the provider. Ellis and Whittington (1988) stress that the basis of quality assurance in human services is the competence and social interaction skills of the service provider, but a vital element is the possession of a set of "caring attitudes" on the part of the service staff, which motivate their interactions, and are visible to the consumers through the style and pattern of these interactions. These attitudes in turn have their root in the personal values held by the service staff, and the corporate values of the service as a whole.

Human Service Values

The values and service philosophies mentioned above form, as we have suggested, one of the salient features of human services. In other service industries, the predominant values are generally in two areas: providing a service for customers and making a profit. It is not often that you find a service industry that operates on a value system that stresses altruism, spiritual development or the relief of human suffering. By contrast, most human services have such "higher" ideals as their basic philosophy, whether or not this is articulated in a formal way by the organisation concerned. Most of these ideals are forms of social welfare ideologies that have influenced service provision for the last century, in one form or another. These ideologies themselves have, in turn, their root in the stereotypes and perceptions we hold of people and society in general, and of disabled or dysfunctional individuals in particular. Wolfensberger (1972) lists the most common stereotyped perceptions in society concerning the group he terms "devalued people", who form the bulk of the consumers of human services, at least in the mental health, disability and social services fields. These include "the eternal child", animal and vegetable analogies and being seen as objects of ridicule.

Dalley (1988, 1992) discusses the way in which general social welfare ideologies influence service provision. She distinguished two competing ideologies that characterise most modern social welfare value systems: possessive individualism and collectivism. The second of these is the basis for the present welfare state and human services provided through it—free health care, social service, disability benefits, etc.—and has been the motivating philosophy since the last century. It combines the motives of altruism and charity, with the emphasis on collective expressions of social responsibility. It also encompasses the principle of egalitarianism and equity: all are equal and should therefore have equal access to human services. The other ideology—possessive individualism—stresses personal freedom, privacy and rights. Dalley points out that this finds its expression in the notion of the nuclear family as an ideal model of society, and that this model is the foundation for the pattern of care advocated in many of the social welfare organisations mentioned above. When care, support or professional input is required, and the immediate nuclear family cannot provide it, then the human service offered should resemble the family model as closely as possible, and should adopt the same value systems, corresponding to possessive individualism. This leads to human service values that stress care in the community, personal rights and choice.

To the two human service ideologies recognised by Dalley, three more might be added. The first of these is that of education—the philosophy that all may be improved through the proper application of an educational process. This idea has its origins in the Enlightenment, and found early expression in the humanitarian work of the founders of training schools for what we would now term developmentally disabled children—Itard, Seguin and

Guggenbühl. Ryan and Thomas (1987) review their work, and stress that the work of these pioneers in education influenced not only the education of handicapped children, but also the mainstream education of all children, with its emphasis on compulsory education, and the general advancement of society through increased educational opportunities. Another ideology therefore might be the development of the individual through education and training.

The second additional ideology is that of the medical model. This has been mentioned before in the context of Wolfensberger's description of the stereotypes underlying value systems. It is a strong and pervasive ideology that has had a major influence both directly and indirectly on human services for many groups. Based on the medical principle of the sanctity of human life and the need to reduce suffering, it has directly influenced services through its adoption not only by the medical profession but also by other similar associated groups such as nursing, physiotherapy, occupational therapy and clinical psychology. The medical model stresses the pathology of the person, and focuses attention on a dysfunctional part of the person that can be made functional again through the application of treatment. At its worst it combines paternalism and moral authoritarianism to produce increased dependence on the part of the "patient", a result to which Illich (1976) has drawn attention. The medical, pathological view of human needs has also indirectly influenced other human services, including social services and education. In many services, the person is secondary to their problem, which is the source of referral into the system, the focus of assessment and treatment, and ultimately of their conceptualisation within the system.

The last of the additional ideologies is the most recent, and is presently having a large impact on human services for many groups, particularly those with physical disability and learning disability. The philosophy of normalisation was first developed in Scandinavia, but was developed by Wolfensberger (1972), who later termed it "social role valorisation" (Wolfensberger, 1983). Wolfensberger assumes that many people who use human services are devalued by society, partly by implicit stereotypes and their accompanying value and belief systems (to which we have already referred) and by the service itself, in terms of the service philosophy or model on which it operates, the methods it uses and the image it projects of the people concerned. He defines social role valorisation as:

> the creation, support and defence of valued social roles for people who are at risk of devaluation. (Wolfensberger, 1983, p. 234)

There are seven core themes identified that are the basis of the principle of normalisation (Wolfensberger and Thomas, 1983):

1. Many social value systems operate at an unconscious level, and are not articulated by the service providers, but still are a powerful influence on the attitudes of staff within the service. In order to change the quality of the service provided, it is necessary to articulate and if necessary change the value system on which the service and staff operate.

2. The behaviour of people served by the service is profoundly influenced by the expectancies and roles placed on them by the staff of the service, and by society in general. Being cast into a particular (devalued) social role results in the person fulfilling the expectancies associated with that role. The goal of quality services should be the introduction and development of valued social roles for the people they serve.

3. A relationship exists between the number of devaluing characteristics a person possesses and the image or impact they have on society. For example, the more able you are, the more you can exhibit minor devaluing characteristics such as odd behaviour. The principle of normalisation suggests that human services should err on the side of conservatism (the so-called "conservatism corollary") so that they should attempt to overcompensate for devaluing characteristics, and establish the highest possible quality of service.

4. Normalisation stresses the developmental model of human functioning, so that any person may grow, change and develop as a result of opportunities. High quality services should therefore provide such opportunities for individual development.

5. Modelling is a powerful tool in the development of human behaviour, and high quality human services should therefore model patterns of behaviour and interaction that increase the valued roles of their clients.

6. Human services make statements about how they view their clients, and about their characteristics, through the images they employ and public statements they make. Much of this operates at an unconscious level, by associative mechanisms. High quality services should always employ positive imagery when portraying their clients.

7. In order to provide opportunities for the development of valued social roles, and to influence public perceptions, devalued people should be integrated into the community and wider society and not segregated in groups. This requires the use not only of generic services, but also of highly valued activities and settings.

Like many of the ideologies on which human services operate, normalisation has its challengers and critics (see for example Brown and Smith, 1992). But its influence is wide, perhaps because it subsumes most of the positive aspects of the other ideologies, and provides an alternative view to the medical model, particularly in the field of mental health and disabilities. Many of the criticisms concern the difficulty of the language in which the principles are expressed, and as a result, many human services have adopted a formulation of the principles set out by John O'Brien, and known as the "Five Service Accomplishments" (O'Brien, 1987). This approach is of great relevance in the context of this book, as it has as its basis the development of human services and what they should attempt to accomplish for their clients. The five accomplishments are:

1. *Community presence*: the people served must show their actual physical presence in the wider community, using the same facilities as everyone else. Service should support users in achieving this.

2. *Choice*: services users should be supported in making choices about their lives and presented with meaningful options in small everyday matters and major life decisions.

3. *Competence*: services should enable users to develop useful skills and attributes that will enhance their functioning within the community and develop valued characteristics and roles.

4. *Respect*: services should enhance the social role of people they serve by affording them respect and treating them with dignity,

and developing a positive image through providing opportunities for choosing valued forms of dress, activities and environments.

5. *Participation*: services should enable users to participate fully in the life of the community and should support the development and maintenance of natural relationships with their families, peers and neighbours.

The formulations of normalisation by both Wolfensberger and O'Brien have been used by them to devise service evaluation and assessment tools for human services. We will consider these in Chapter 5, where we review evaluation methods.

The Influence of Values on Quality

Earlier it was suggested that the key to quality in human service lies in the fundamental "moment of truth"—the interaction between service provider and service consumer. In turn the nature of this interaction is influenced not only by the expectations and perceptions of the consumer, but more importantly—in terms of the quality of the service—by the service provider. Their behaviour will be the result of a set of values, attitudes and stereotypes about the consumer and their use of the service, as well as professional or vocational training and job specifications. Peters and Waterman (1982) consider an explicit set of values of one the determining factors for excellence in an industry. They say:

> Every excellent company we studied is clear on what it stands for, and takes the process of value shaping seriously. In fact, we wonder whether it is possible to be an excellent company without clarity on values and without having the right sort of values. (Peters and Waterman, 1982, p. 280)

They also report that value systems are rarely transmitted through formal written procedures, but through myths, stories and actions. The excellent companies they describe lead them to identify a number of ways in which these value systems lead to quality and excellence. Firstly, they are stated in qualitative, not quantitative terms. Secondly, they serve as a means of inspiring everyone in the company, from top to bottom, and thirdly, they are present in the way that people relate to each other within the company, as well as to the customers. The message Peters and Waterman seek to convey is that quality and excellence follow from a clear correct set of values that pervades the whole service enterprise.

John O'Brien (1990), in a discussion on the basis of quality residential services for people with learning disability, points out that the value system of an organisation is linked to two concepts that in turn determine quality: leadership and vision. Leadership is the process of setting and maintaining value systems for the organisation, demonstrating them to all concerned through statements and actions and motivating others in the service to develop and employ the same systems for the benefit of the clients or consumers of the service. The vision is the inspiration that comes from employing the value system and seeking to use it to animate and direct staff into providing quality services.

One of the crucial aspects in determining the quality of human services is therefore to be found in the personal and corporate value systems of the organisation. The problem for developing and managing services is how to instil such systems and ensure that the actions of staff are coherent with them. This might be done by the process of staff selection. Davidow and Uttal (1989) suggest that this is one of the main ways in which services offering high quality customer service maintain and develop this amongst their staff. Such services will select staff on the basis of their articulated values, or will tend to recruit self- selected staff who are drawn to work in that organisation because of the match between the corporate values and their own personal values. In the field of human services, training is seen as the most important method of developing values. Lindley and Wainwright (1992) discuss the issue of training in the values of normalisation, and the crucial question of whether this type of value development amounts to indoctrination or pseudo-religious conversion, and Georgiades and Phillimore (1975) remind us of the ineffectiveness of skills training, per se, in producing lasting attitude change. In other situations, attitude change has been the subject of specific interventions, and the literature of organisational change shows that a prerequisite for the introduction of such change is the "unfreezing" of old attitudes, the introduction of new ones and "refreezing" to ensure that they are instilled.

Whatever method is used to maintain value systems in human services, the crucial factor is ensuring that the staff operate at all times on the basis of these systems, or least in a manner that is coherent with them. This concerns their interactions not only with consumers, but also with others involved in the service, such as colleagues and other professionals. In a community mental health team, for example, it is essential that team members operate from the same values base in terms of interactions with clients, their relatives and other disciplines and agencies that may be involved in the case. One way in which this can be done is through the various techniques of total quality management, which later we will consider in depth.

MODELS OF QUALITY IN HUMAN SERVICES

In the second part of this chapter we will continue the process of narrowing our focus of discussion. We will look at some of the specific ways in which quality has been approached in a major human service area, that of health and disability care in its widest aspects. At the same time we will relate this to the work on service industry quality that we have already discussed in this and the previous chapter. The area that we will examine is the one in which most therapeutic professions operate, so lastly we will examine the relevance of the models outlined to these professional groups.

Defining Quality in Health Care Services

If defining quality is difficult in relation to service industries as a whole, and even more difficult in relation to human services, then defining quality in health care services is fraught with difficulty. There is also an initial problem of defining what health care is. This has been addressed recently in the context of defining "health" and "social" care in the new community care management arrangements in Great Britain. The official government line is that health care needs are those needs of any individual that can only be met by medically-led qualified health care staff, but the ambiguities of this definition make it an unworkable one in practice. Health care comprises and represents a broad spectrum of activities, carried out by many different professions and trades, across a variety of types of situation for an infinite variety of consumers. The only unifying factors are the desired outcomes which include the development of health-related behaviours, the alleviation of suffering and the furtherance of human development. In an attempt to clarify the problems of definition of quality, Vuori (1982) describes three ways of defining the quality of health care services that are apparent from a review of the literature on quality assurance in this field. These three ways are: nominal definition, content analysis and operational definition. The first of these tries to produce a universal, all-embracing, logically coherent definition that will fit all situations and consumers. The failure of this type of approach led Vuori to conclude that there will probably never be a single comprehensive definition of quality health care services that could be used to measure the quality of consumer care. As a result, he reports that many writers have considered content analysis a more fruitful approach, where quality is seen as a multicomponent entity, with each component separable and definable. This type of approach has a number of examples, and is related to the type of approach we have already examined above for service industries in general. The last method is to adopt an operational definition that suits the context in which it is applied and does not seek to be universally applicable. Quality is therefore defined by the tools used to measure it—quality is what you see. The problem with this type of approach is that, as Donabedian (1966) has suggested, the definition of quality might be anything you want it to be. Vuori states finally:

> It may be impossible to develop a definition that would satisfy all its users. As a consequence, every user of the concept should clearly spell out what he means by quality: quality for whom, quality defined by whom, quality for what purpose, and which aspect of quality. (Vuori, 1983, p. 35)

Pfeffer (1992) thinks that there are four meanings of quality in human services. The first of these is the popular meaning, that of luxury and advantage. This is out of place in the realm of health and social care, where need and equity are prominent concepts. The second meaning is that of scientific performance, where quality is based on measurement, control and inspection. This is also alien to human services, as it promotes a closed system with the power in the hands of professionals, and in which the user or consumer is not involved or able to participate. The third meaning is that of excellence, which is based on the customer service approach to quality. Here quality is a constant striving to meet customer expectations, with all staff involved in furthering this aim. Pfeffer criticises this approach on the grounds that it has two main problems. The first of these is the lack of evidence on the relationship of customer satisfaction to success in the public sector. In other service industries, as we have seen, this relationship is axiomatic. In most human, public services, however, there is little need to satisfy customers, and often large disincentives to doing so. If a good service attracts more customers, in the public sector with finite and limited resources, this can lead to organisational, financial and political problems. Fourthly, there is the consumerist approach to quality, which relies on the market forces of the choosing consumer to regulate quality. The problem here is one already mentioned, the difficulty experienced by consumers in exercising real choice in human services. Consumers are not empowered. In public services they do not have the necessary financial control to be so.

Components of Quality Health Care Services

Intuitively there are some aspects of any health care service that would seem to be basically desirable conditions for the provision of quality health care. Firstly, the health care delivered must be effective in alleviating suffering and creating better health, as this is its sole reason for existence. Does the service actually achieve anything in terms of making people better? This concept is similar to that which was discussed in our overall review of the definition of quality in the last chapter—"fitness for use". As with manufactured products, the service product, health care, must actually do what it is supposed to do. Secondly, the service must be efficient in its use of resources, particularly given the unlimited nature of the demand for health care, and the financial conditions under which most human services operate, as we have described above. In the discussions of quality in general in Chapter 2, we saw how quality has a cost component, which is equally true of health care services. Thirdly, it must create confidence amongst its clients by competence in performance and operation. Health care is an area in which most people must have enough trust and confidence in their health care practitioners, particularly physicians and surgeons, to allow them to carry out invasive and often painful diagnostic and treatment procedures, and to trust them with their most basic asset—life itself. In this there is similarity to the ideas on service quality listed above, where customer confidence, trust and security are vital elements.

These intuitive notions of what constitutes a quality health care service not only correspond with mainstream industrial ideas on quality, and specifically those on service industry quality, but also appear in various forms in most of the influential writing on the definition of the components of quality health care. Interestingly, much of the writing on health care quality has come from within the field, with often little reference to ideas and methods outwith it. Although this has given rise to a somewhat isolationist feel to some of the literature, many of the same concepts appear, which is perhaps not surprising, given that health care is after all just another form of service industry, however much some practitioners dislike this fact.

There are a number of systems of definition in health care services. The American Public Health Association (Myers, 1969) specified four essential elements of good care:

1. *Accessibility*: the possibility of a consumer obtaining the services he or she needs at a time and place where and when they are needed, in sufficient amounts and at reasonable cost (or free). The three measurable dimensions are personal accessibility, comprehensiveness of services and quantitative adequacy.

2. *Quality*: the level of application to the care provided of the most up-to-date and effective practices and technology. Measurable dimensions include professional competence, personal acceptability and qualitative adequacy.

3. *Continuity*: the treatment of a consumer as a whole person in an integrated way under the guidance of a central source of care. Measurable aspects include person-centred care, the existence of a central source of care and coordination of services.

4. *Efficiency*: the relationship between the impact of the service and its costs. Measurable components include the existence of equitable financing, adequate compensation for negligence and efficient administration and management.

To these elements the APHA adds a fifth area of measurement—consumer and provider satisfaction—which is defined as consumer satisfaction with the service, providers and outcome of health care, and as provider satisfaction with working conditions. A similar addition is made by Donabedian (1980), who distinguishes between the scientific–professional aspects and the interpersonal aspects, with both being important in assessing quality. In discussing these dimensions, Vuori (1982) suggests that they may be simplified to four main dimensions: effectiveness, efficiency, scientific–technical quality and adequacy.

The same dimensions appear in the work of two British writers who have had a major influence on the definition of quality within the British National Health Service. Robert Maxwell, in an article in the *British Medical Journal* in 1984, outlines six dimensions of quality health care:

1. Access to services—ease of accessing the system, physical accessibility and length of waiting time.
2. Relevance to need—for the whole community and its health care needs.
3. Effectiveness—for individual consumers, including technical competence.
4. Equity (fairness)—availability equally to all in relation to need.
5. Social acceptability—including physical and interpersonal aspects, and the ethical nature of treatment procedures.
6. Efficiency and economy—relating outcome to costs and resource use.

Maxwell considers these as examples of the dimensions of quality, and not a definitive list, which might be useful in devising measurement tools to quantitatively measure health care quality.

Charles Shaw (1986) has taken these dimensions and elaborated them as a starting point in the development of quality assurance systems in health care. The definitions he adopts are:

1. Appropriateness—the service or procedure is what the population or individual actually needs.

2. Equity—a fair share is available for all the population.

3. Accessibility—services are not compromised by undue limits of time and distance.

4. Effectiveness—services are achieving the intended benefit for the individual and the population.

5. Acceptability—services are provided such as to satisfy the health expectations of patients, providers and the community.

6. Efficiency—resources are not wasted on one service or patient to the detriment of another.

In this the major element is that of appropriateness, because without it, the health care delivered is irrelevant, and useless, regardless of its other qualities. It must be related to the needs of the person, and to those of the population as a whole.

We have already mentioned in an earlier chapter the approach to quality suggested by Øvretveit (1991). He puts forward three categories of quality, within which there may be subcategories approaching the dimensions listed above. The three types of quality are:

1. *Client quality*: what consumers want from the service, individually and as a population.

2. *Professional quality*: whether the service meets the needs as defined by professionals and whether it correctly carries out techniques and procedures that are believed necessary to meet consumer needs.

3. *Management quality*: the most efficient and productive use of resources to meet consumer needs within limits and directives set by higher authorities.

Øvretveit uses this threefold definition to construct systems of quality assurance and relates each to methods. Client quality is ensured by consumer satisfaction measures and techniques. Professional quality is ensured by standard setting and the process of clinical, professional or organisational audit. Lastly, management quality is concerned with the development of a total quality management approach that internalises the values and competencies of a quality approach in the system.

Table 2 Donabedian's dimensions of quality in health care measurement.

	Structure	Process	Outcome
Definition	Increases or decreases the probability of good performance	Normative behaviour, valued for its contribution to valued consequences, or for higher principles	Change in patient's current and future health status attributable to antecedent health care
Examples	Any relatively stable characteristic of health care providers Physical setting Organisational setting Resources Equipment	Interpersonal process Technical care Competence of staff Care processes	Morbidity Mortality Social functioning Psychological state Health-related knowledge

Finally, one of the most vital ideas on quality in health care services, and particularly its measurement, comes from the work of Avis Donabedian, best summarised in his 1980 paper, which we have already cited above. This is not a definitional system as such, but more an approach to measurement, and a delineation of the essential aspects of a health care system that need to be considered in any quantitative system of quality assurance or development. There are three aspects to his system: structure, process and outcome. Table 2 gives the definition and examples of each of these.

Each of these three elements is an essential part of any adequate description of the quality of a health care system, and of any methodology for the assessment of quality. They form the foundation for various systems of accreditation, clinical audit and monitoring, which we will consider in later chapters, and the basis for many systems of health care quality assurance.

CHAPTER 4   Quality assurance

QUALITY ASSURANCE AND CONTROL TECHNIQUES

If, as we have seen, defining quality in industry, service industries and human services is a difficult operation, then this is paralleled by the difficulty in defining quality assurance in the same contexts. In this chapter we will examine firstly the nature of quality assurance and control in the general field of industry, including a brief review of BS5750/ISO9000, and also an overview of the most common techniques for quality control. Lastly we will look at the logical extension of quality assurance, total quality management. This will act as a background to the next two chapters, where we will review the same topics as they have been, or could be, applied to health and social care, and the following chapter, where we will discuss quality assurance systems in the context of the therapeutic professions.

In Chapter 2 we examined the historical trends in the development of approaches to quality and excellence, and the progression outlined by Dale, Lascelles and Plunkett (1990) from inspection towards quality control, quality assurance and finally to total quality management. In their four-phase model, quality assurance is the third stage in the evolution of techniques of developing quality. In this book, however, quality assurance is seen as a term for the framework within which a number of methods for the development, evaluation, monitoring and maintenance of quality and excellence are carried out. These methods will include the basic techniques of quality control, the management method which enables these techniques to be employed—total quality management—and the system of evaluation or accreditation within which many quality assurance systems have been developed recently, namely that of the British Standard, BS5750. Indeed the official definition of quality assurance set out in BS5750 states that quality assurance "contains all those planned and systematic actions required to provide adequate confidence that a product or service will satisfy given requirements for quality". This operates within a quality system which is defined in the standard as "the organisational structure, responsibilities, procedures, processes and resources for implementing quality management". Dale and Boaden (1993) have recently presented a revised model of quality assurance, which combines a number of elements into what they term a "total quality framework". Like our definition presented above, this recognises that the development of a coherent approach to quality involves a number of aspects, including using systems and techniques for monitoring quality, measurement tools for setting and monitoring against standards, a management organising function and finally an emphasis on cultural change to establish a quality philosophy throughout the enterprise. We will examine this model in more detail later in the chapter.

The basic elements in quality assurance are straightforward, whatever other embellishments might be added to the term. One of the best descriptions of this activity comes from our main field of discussion, that of health care. The Canadian Council on Hospital Accreditation (1985) defines quality assurance as a five-stage process, comprising:

1. The establishment of functional goals.

2. The implementation of procedures to achieve these goals.

3. The regular assessment of performance relative to goals.

4. The proposal of solutions to close the gap between performance and goal.

5. The documentation and reporting of this assessment activity.

The key elements of this definition, and of most similar ones, are *goal setting*, *assessment*, and *reporting*. Many authors talk of a "quality assurance cycle" in which goals—or standards as is so often used—are set, assessed, performance modified and reported on in a cyclical activity that is constantly renewing. Øvretveit (1991), again in the context of health care, talks of a quality management cycle, which contains a number of specific stages:

1. *Service requirements,* which involve having a clear understanding of the customer's needs, and of the aims, philosophy and values of the service.

2. *Operational specifications,* which transform the service requirements into more detailed service specifications, standards and objectives.

3. *Measurement of performance against specifications,* which involves monitoring against the standards set and adjustment to the processes used to achieve them, or surpass them.

Øvretveit considers that there are two key aspects to the establishment and successful operation of any quality management system, namely the use of quality tools and techniques, and the development of ways of involving all staff throughout the process, that is the implementation of total quality management throughout the organisation.

Before we consider the literature on quality assurance systems in human services in the next chapter, it is worth looking at the main aspects of quality assurance in industry as outlined above. These are the tools and techniques of quality control, the elements of a comprehensive quality assurance system as in BS5750 and lastly, the means to establish this throughout a company, total quality management. In doing this we will also examine how such techniques have been used in service industries in general.

The Tools and Techniques of Quality Control

There are a number of accepted tools and techniques of quality control or assurance that form a part of most quality assurance systems. The underlying theme of all of them is the objective, usually statistical, analysis of features of the production or service process that are important, measurable and changeable. We will review five of them here: Taguchi methods, statistical process control, quality function deployment, quality costing and quality circles.

Taguchi methods

Taguchi has given his name to the most statistical of quality control procedures. A good discussion of the application of Taguchi's ideas is to be found in Disney and Bendall (1990). As we saw in Chapter 2, there are two principal ideas in Taguchi's work. The first of these is his definition of quality in terms of the loss suffered by society when a product does not reach an adequate level of quality. The smaller the loss, the better or more desirable a product is, and so the higher the quality it has. This loss may be expressed as customer dissatisfaction, costs of replacement or repair, loss of market image, and loss of market share. In keeping with his highly statistical approach, Taguchi considers that a product causes this loss not only when it does not meet specification, but also when it deviates from a target value, which he exemplifies with a quadratic equation. It is the customer who experiences this loss, which may be in terms of inconvenience, financial loss or customer goodwill. As the parameter value moves away from the desired target, so the loss increases exponentially. The essential part of this principle is the achievement of quality by the continual reduction in variance. This is achieved by setting a clear target value for the product's performance characteristics, with defined variability around the mean. Once these values are defined, statistically planned experiments should be used to identify those settings of the production process that will reduce the variation in performance.

The second principle in Taguchi's methods is that of "off-line quality control". In each production process there are three stages: product (or service) design, process of production or delivery design and production or delivery itself. Taguchi stresses the need for quality to be built in at the design stage, but also for continual control during the production process to reduce variance at that stage. The "off-line" stage equates to that of design of product and process, whilst the "on-line" stage is that carried out during the process itself.

Taguchi's complex methods relate closely to the statistical approach to quality control, and are ideally suited for tangible production processes, which is reflected in their widespread usage in electrical and electro-mechanical engineering, reviewed by Disney and Bendall.

Statistical process control

Closely related to Taguchi methods are those of statistical process control (SPC). Early work by Deming and Ishikawa ensured that it is now one of the most widely used techniques in quality management systems in manufacturing industry. Oakland (1989) points out that SPC is not just a set of tools, however, but also a quality improvement strategy that is an essential part of a total quality management system.

The basic element of SPC is the collection of data in an objective manner, and its analysis in graphical form to provide the input to a series of improvement processes. The main aim of this improvement is to remove sources of variation in the product or service by the analysis and consideration of that variation. Ishikawa (1985) describes the "seven basic tools" of SPC. These are:

1. *Process flow charting*: this is to outline the operations required in the production of delivery process, and the interrelationships between them.

2. *Check sheets*: these document the frequency of each operation in the process that features on the flow chart.

3. *Histograms*: these are graphical displays of the variations using the data from the first two tools.

4. *Pareto analysis*: using the data from the check sheets, Pareto diagrams rank the principal sources of variation within the production process, leading to a graphical description of the main priority areas for process change.

5. *Cause-and-effect analysis and brainstorming*: the cause-and-effect diagram (also known as an Ishikawa diagram or a fishbone chart) maps the inputs to the process that affect quality at each stage of that process. In a group setting, brainstorming techniques around the problem as depicted in the above charts can lead to the identification of potential causes and solutions.

6. *Scatter diagrams*: these establish the relationship between two factors or parameters affecting the production or delivery process.

7. *Control charts*: these usually plot the mean and range of a product variability over time or the course of the production process. There are a wide range of charts in use, and some examples appear in Shaw and Dale (1990).

Ceridwen (1992) surveyed 40 US companies recognised for their expertise in quality matters and found that the top five of the above tools identified as used most frequently were:

1. Flow charting.

2. Cause-and-effect diagrams.

3. Pareto charts.

4. Control charts.

5. Scatter diagrams.

The companies involved saw the use of these techniques as essential aspects of the overall quality control system. Shaw and Dale (1990) carried out a survey of suppliers of automotive parts using SPC, and found that, although the methods were seen as useful tools to improve the quality of the finished product, there were major difficulties experienced by many users in the introduction of SPC and its use. These difficulties included lack of knowledge about SPC, poor understanding of SPC within the company, practical difficulties in applying SPC to a particular process, and choosing and using relevant charts. The authors discuss two main categories of difficulty: lack of management commitment and lack of practical knowledge and confidence to use SPC. Again as stated above, the main advantage of SPC is in the graphical methods of data presentation, as part of a total approach to quality improvement.

Quality function deployment

Quality function deployment is another technique that uses statistical analysis and graphical presentation, with the aim of forming a system for:

> translating consumer requirements into appropriate company requirements at every stage, from research, through product design and development to manufacture, distribution, installation and marketing, sales and service. (American Supplier Institute, 1987)

The emphasis of this technique is on the whole of the design, production and delivery process, so that quality is built in to all parts of the procedure. Using the tools does not guarantee improved quality; they must form part of an overall quality system, and their use can lead on the employment of statistical process control to look at the specific aspects of the production process, as outlined above. A good review is contained in Burn (1990).

Oakland (1989) states that there are "seven new tools" of quality control that form the set of techniques labelled quality function deployment, and he gives excellent examples of their use in manufacturing industry. The seven tools are:

1. *Affinity diagram*: this is a form of brainstorming, where graphical means are used to gather large amounts of ideas, opinions and issues concerning the quality of a product into groupings based on natural relationships between these items.

2. *Interrelationship digraph*: this graphical technique takes one of the groups of issues identified from an affinity diagram and maps out the logical or sequential links amongst related factors concerning that issue.

3. *Systems flow/tree diagram*: this is a form of flow chart that maps out a full range of activities or operations that must be performed in order to obtain a desired or set objective. The emphasis is on using the data from the above two techniques to give the input to a more operationally related stage of analysis.

4. *Matrix diagram*: this formalises the interrelationships and correlations between tasks, function, characteristics and customer requirements to show their relative importance. The matrices may be "L-shaped", where data are presented in row and column format, combined into a "T-shaped" matrix which covers more complex relationships amongst multiple data sets, or entered into a complicated diagram called the "house of quality" (because it looks like a house!), which charts multiple relationships.

5. *Matrix data analysis*: this takes one or more of the relationships amongst data shown in the types of matrix outlined above and simplifies them onto a simple x and y axes chart.

6. *Process decision programme chart*: this attempts to map out graphically each event and contingency that might occur whilst

considering a quality improvement item constructed from the above methods. The aim is to anticipate the unexpected within the process, and plan for it.

7. *Arrow diagram*: the basic element in scheduling an operation, this maps out actions over time, and as such is similar to a "Gantt chart" used in project planning techniques.

The above techniques lend themselves to a particular stage of the process of production, where an item is being designed, and the manufacturing process that produces it is being installed. The techniques are much "softer" than those of statistical process control, and are suited to use by multidisciplinary teams in a cooperative work situation. Burn states:

> Quality Function deployment is best thought of as a systematic approach to identifying and recording areas for priority action, to indicating where the use of other procedures and techniques, e.g. the Taguchi method of experimental design, will achieve most benefit in relation to the customer's perceived needs. (Burn, 1990, p. 87)

Quality costing

Quality costing attempts to improve quality through a realistic quantification of these costs, and attribution of the costs to various aspects of the production process. As with the other techniques it forms part of an overall approach to quality management, and is the topic of its own British Standard, BS6143—"Guide to the determination and use of quality related costs", which appeared in 1981. As with other financial information, quality costs are able to be budgeted, measured and analysed. There are a number of types of elements that can constitute quality costs:

1. *Internal failure costs*: these occur when things go wrong in the production process, and items fail to reach quality standards and criteria. Types of internal failure costs include: wastage costs, scrapping costs, reworking costs, reinspection costs, downgrading costs and the cost of failure analysis.

2. *External failure costs*: these costs occur after production and sale, and are often detected by the customer after delivery. Types of

external failure costs might include: repair costs, warranty claim costs, costs of handling complaints, cost of returns, legal liability costs and possible litigation costs.

3. *Appraisal costs*: these costs are associated with the inspection, evaluation and monitoring of the production process and materials to ensure conformance with specified quality standards. The types of costs included in this category might be: inspection costs, quality audit costs and the cost of purchasing specialist inspection equipment.

4. *Prevention costs*: these are costs associated with the implementation of a quality assurance system, and its maintenance, and might include costs of quality audits, quality design processes and training.

Once such quality costs are identified, they can be used to illustrate, usually graphically, to an organisation the value of producing a quality product, and can be managed through a quality management process. The best text on this topic is by Dale and Plunkett (1991), and good descriptions and case studies are to be found in Plunkett and Dale (1990). Dale (1986) suggests that the four categories listed above are not mutually exclusive, which can lead to difficulties in cost apportionment, but that in most organisations, the costs of quality can range between 10 and 20% of annual turnover. The advantages of using quality costing approaches in service industries, Dale implies, are the expression of quality-related activities in cash terms, the establishment of evidence for quality improvement by the demonstration of the costs of waste, the ability to make comparisons with other organisations, and the ability to make business decisions on quality costs in an objective manner.

Quality circles

The last technique of quality management that we will examine is one which has gained a "vogue" following in industry over the last few years. The techniques of quality assurance that make up quality function deployment, as described earlier in this chapter, are "softer" in their approach to quality than others similarly discussed, such as statistical process control. This is because they focus less on the data analysis side of quality improvement, and more on the interpersonal processes involved in attempting to assure and control quality in an organisation. Quality circles are a logical extension to this softer approach, as they explicitly attempt to use group processes to generate change and influence organisational relationships. There are a number of texts on quality circles, such as those by Hutchins (1985), Robson (1982, 1984) and Barra (1989), which describe the methodology in detail, but also suffer from an over-enthusiastic, even evangelical approach to the use of this technique, which has led to unrealistic expectations on the part of management for the effect of quality circles on the quality process.

There are a number of basic factors in quality circles and their development. Barra describes four such factors:

1. Quality circles enable workers to participate in the improvement of their products and their jobs, so building pride in their product and a sense of participation in, and belonging to, the organisation.

2. Quality circles recognise and use the intellectual and practical potential of all the employees of an organisation, and provide a safe framework within which such contributions can be made.

3. Quality circles provide training and structured opportunities for staff to become involved in the interpersonal processes within the organisation that lead to joint problem solving. The circles are employee-owned and allow for personal development and growth, together with allowing a sense of achievement at work.

4. Quality circles flourish best in, and promote, a democratic, participative and person-orientated management style that values two-way communication and values the contribution of all employees to the functioning of the organisation.

Quality circles originated in Japan in the early 1960s, and have since been promulgated on a worldwide basis, with a rapid growth in the early 1980s. A quality circle is defined with deceptive ease. Lees and Dale (1990) quote a Japanese brochure on quality circles, which gives this definition:

A small group which acts spontaneously within the same area to perform quality control activities. This small group will continuously, as part of the company-wide quality control activity, conduct self and mutual improvement and performance control and improvement of their workplace using QC techniques with all members' participation. (Lees and Dale, 1990, p. 244)

Oakland (1989) similarly provides a short definition of the essentials of quality circles, which are groups of workers who meet voluntarily, regularly, in normal working time, under the leadership of their "supervisor" to identify, analyse and solve work-related problems and to recommend solutions to management. These solutions should then be implemented by the workers who form the circle. As part of their approach to problem solving, quality circles may draw on other techniques of quality assurance and control, including some of the problem-solving tools of quality function deployment and the statistical and graphical analysis tools of statistical process control.

There have been a number of critical papers concerning quality circles, particularly highlighting the over-enthusiastic approaches of their devotees, and the issue of quality circle failure. Some of these arguments are summarised in Lees and Dale (1990) and Dale (1986), who also highlight some of the necessary conditions for quality circle success. These include the need for circles to be organised in the context of, and suited to, the organisational culture of the company. They function best within a culture and management style that stresses participation and a management philosophy of encouraging communication with employees, and where they are an integral, but not exclusive, part of a total quality system. There are instances, however, as Lees and Dale point out from their extensive survey work on quality circles in British industry, where circles can work within an autocratic management structure, if their prime purpose is one of responsibility for quality improvement.

Another necessary component in quality circle success is the consideration of their own organisational structure. The use of a skilled facilitator seems to be a recognised vital ingredient in successful functioning. The two articles quoted earlier give extensive discussion on quality circles and their relative success or failure as a technique. Dale (1986) discusses the use of quality circles in service industries, with data from a survey of a number of service companies. His work again stresses the importance of a facilitator, and reports a number of benefits, including the opportunity to become involved in the organisation, better teamwork and increased job satisfaction. Drawbacks identified in service industries include the intangibility of the topics tackled by the circle (see earlier discussions on the nature of service industries); the time necessary for meeting as a circle, where service industry personnel are more likely to be in a direct client-contact relationship than counterparts in manufacturing industry; greater turnover in staff in service industries and few models on which to base actions, particularly in Britain.

Barrick and Alexander (1987) have reviewed the research on the efficacy of quality circles, and suggest that there is a positive-effects bias. In a more recent paper (Barrick and Alexander, 1992), the same authors suggest that the implementation of quality circles is based less on research finding such as Dale's, and more on pragmatic management considerations. They outline a technique for assessing the benefits of quality circles called utility analysis, and show that, using this statistical method, the quantification of the magnitude of the effect of quality circles, at least on the financial performance of the organisation as cited in some papers, is far more complex than suggested. They also stress that the justification for using quality circles may be best made in terms of improved employee motivation and better attitudes, rather than pure financial considerations.

Conclusions

The descriptions of the various quality control and assurance techniques given above have shown that there are a number of ways in which quality can be improved throughout an organisation. They range from analytically based objective tools to the manipulation of interpersonal and group processes. These techniques and tools, as much research suggests, are best seen as merely components of an overall approach to quality assurance, and elements in a larger framework. Ultimately they form constituents of a total approach to quality that we will consider later in this chapter. Before that we will examine a framework with which a total approach to quality can be developed, that of BS5750/ISO9000.

DEVELOPING A QUALITY MANAGEMENT SYSTEM—BS5750/ISO9000

Throughout this book we have referred at times to the British Standard on quality systems, BS5750/ISO9000. This was originally introduced in 1979, with the intention of standardising the requirements for quality systems in manufacturing industries, and giving guidance on the basic criteria for establishing and maintaining such a quality system within an organisation. BS5750/ISO9000 consists of a number of parts or sections, some of which offer general guidance on the application of the standard, while others describe the modification of the standard for certain sectors of manufacturing industry. Recently the version that forms Part 8 has appeared specifically for service industries (British Standards Institute, 1991). Confusion exists with the numbers listed above and those of the ISO version, which differs only in titles and not in content, and the relevant number of the version for service industries is ISO9004-2. The introduction and development of the standards have been mirrored by increasing demand by organisations and companies for accreditation under it. Very few weeks go by in my local newspaper when there is not a report of another local concern gaining accreditation under BS5750/ISO9000, ranging from printers to garages to engineering suppliers. The most recent estimate is that some 13 000 companies, including public and private sector, and manufacturing and service industries, have accreditation under this standard (*Daily Telegraph*, 5 February 1993). There are also an increasing number of publications relating to it, amongst the best, most useful and understandable being those by Swinson (1992), Hall (1992) and Robertson (1992). The first and last of these are particularly relevant to service industries, focusing on accountancy and nursing respectively.

The process of accreditation involves firstly undertaking the necessary preparation, in order to install the quality system along the lines given in the standard. Many firms employ quality consultants to do this, often with the aid of government funds. The main element of this preparation is the production of the quality manual (see Hall, 1992, for an example), and the specification of the procedures for quality control. When it is considered that the firm is sufficiently well prepared, a "third party agency" is contacted or contracted to carry out the assessment. Such agencies are companies that specialise in the assessment of BS5750/ISO9000, and are in themselves registered and accredited with the British Standards Institute to carry these out. There are about 20 such companies in the United Kingdom, some of which specialise in certain market sectors (for example the Quality Scheme for Ready Mixed Concrete), or have specific experience with certain types of organisation. Matching up a third party agency with the organisation to be assessed requires great care, and may not always hinge on price.

THE CERTIFICATION PROCESS

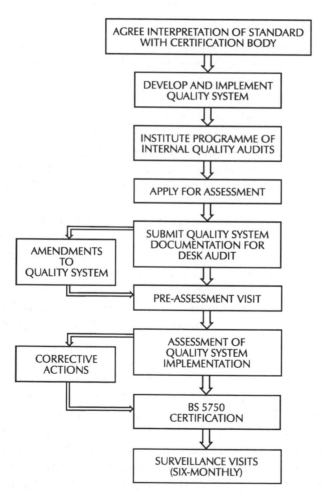

Figure 1   BS5750 accreditation process

The accreditation process involves a sequence of activities, as shown in Figure 1.

The assessment visit by a trained assessment team from the third party agency, led by a "lead assessor", will include examination of records, interviews with staff, observation of procedures in action and possibly interviews with customers. At the end of this procedure, a discussion will take place in which any areas for remedial action will be noted, or at which it will be agreed that a certificate will be issued. Registration is subject to annual renewal, with up to four annual inspections being carried out by the third party agency. There is considerable cost involved, not only in the initial assessment, but also in annual renewal fees.

As this book is concerned with what can be considered to be a type of service industry, we will refer mainly to BS5750/ISO9000 in the version outlined for service industries. There are a number of premises upon which BS5750/ISO9000 Part 8 is based. These include the fact that the standard can be applied to any service industry quality system, whether this is an established service or one in the design stage. Secondly, it covers all those processes required to provide an effective service, including marketing and delivery, and also includes an analysis of the service received by customers. Thirdly, the standard is applicable to all services regardless of size, and similarly, regardless of complexity. Fourthly, the customer will be the ultimate recipient of the service, and will be external to the service. In larger and more complex organisations, however, there are often internal customers for parts of the service (e.g. human resources, finance, etc.), and the standard should also be applicable within the context of these relationships. Fifthly, the service delivery characteristics might be quantitative and measurable or, because of the human nature of services, qualitative or comparable. Within each service there will be elements of both, and many qualitative characteristics subjectively evaluated by customers might be translated into quantitative characteristics that can be measured by the service. (For example, waiting times—subjectively experienced by the customers, but also measurable in quantitative terms by the service.) In the light of these factors, BS5750/ISO9000 seeks to encourage service industries to manage and organise the quality aspects of their service in a more effective way, and recognises that a failure to meet set quality objectives has consequences for the service, in that customers, the service and society in general may be adversely affected. The ultimate responsibility to meet these objectives, and avoid the adverse conditions, is that of management. Therefore the standard encourages a systematic approach to quality management, with the aim of meeting customer needs. This in turn requires a demonstrated commitment to quality principles at all levels of the service organisation, and a continual review of the quality system based heavily on the customers' perception of the service. The standard assumes that the successful application of such an organised approach to quality systems management will bring about improved service performance, in terms of customer satisfaction and financial efficiency. At the same time, the human interactional aspects of services must be accommodated within the standard and the system which it encourages. This is done by managing the social processes involved in service delivery, regarding human interactions as the crucial part of service quality, recognising the importance of customer perceptions, expectations and satisfaction in measuring service quality, recognising the skills and capabilities of the service personnel and therefore motivating them to improve quality in their interactions with customers.

In setting out a framework for quality systems in service industries, BS5750/ISO9000, Part 8 suggests that there are two aspects to be considered, the first of which is the "quality system principles", which are the basic elements upon which the quality system is managed. There are four main elements to any such system:

- Management responsibility
- Quality systems structure
- Personnel and material resources
- Interface with customers

These are all interrelated, with the central element being the last, the interface with customers. Under each of these four elements, there are a number of subelements that comprise and clarify the main element. The second aspect is the way in which these principles are put into practice, that is the "quality system operational elements", which will vary far more than the quality system principles with the different nature of the service or its constituent parts. The following are the main elements or sections of BS5750/

ISO9000, Part 8. Within each element there are numerous sections and subsections. Readers are referred to the BSI publication for the detail of these, but we have maintained the outline numbering system of BS5750/ISO9000 below.

5. Quality System Principles

5.2 Management responsibility
Management is responsible for establishing a policy for service quality and customer satisfaction. Successful implementation of this policy is dependent on management commitment to the development and effective operation of a quality system.

5.3 Personnel and material resource
Management should provide sufficient and appropriate resources to implement the quality system and achieve the quality objectives.

5.4 Quality system structure
The service organisation should develop, establish, document, implement and maintain a quality system as a means by which stated policies and objectives for service quality may be accomplished. The operational elements of a quality system are described in clause 6. The quality system elements should be structured to establish adequate control and assurance over all operational procedures affecting service quality. The quality system should emphasise preventive actions that avoid the occurrence of problems while not sacrificing the ability to respond to and correct failures, should they occur.

5.5 Interface with customers
Management should establish effective interaction between customers and the service organisation's personnel. This is crucial to the quality of the service perceived by the customer. Management can influence this perception by creating an appropriate image based on the reality of actions taken to meet customer needs. This image, presented by personnel at all levels, has a primary effect on the service organisation's relationship with the customer. Personnel with direct customer contact are an important source of information for the ongoing quality improvement process. Management should regularly review the methods used for promoting contacts with customers.

6. Quality System Operational Elements

6.1 Marketing process

6.2 Design process
The process of designing a service involves converting the service brief into specifications for both the service and its delivery and control, while reflecting the organisation's options (i.e. aims, policies and costs). The service

specification defines the service to be provided, whereas the service delivery specification defines the means and methods used to deliver the service. The quality control specification defines the procedures for evaluating and controlling the service and service delivery characteristics. Design of the service specification, the service delivery specification and quality control specification are interdependent and interact throughout the design process. Flow charts are a useful method to depict all activities, relationships and interdependences. The principles of quality control should be applied to the design process itself.

6.3 Service delivery process
Management should assign specific responsibilities to all personnel implementing the service delivery process, including supplier assessment and customer assessment. The provision of a service to a customer entails adherence to the prescribed service delivery specification, monitoring that the service specification is met and adjusting the process when deviations occur.

6.4 Service performance analysis and improvement
A continual evaluation of the operation of the service processes should be practised to identify and actively pursue opportunities for service quality improvement. To implement such evaluations, management should establish and maintain an information system for the collection and dissemination of data from all relevant sources. Management should assign responsibilities for the information system and for service quality improvement.

Advantages and Disadvantages of BS5750/ISO9000

As already stated, there has been a widespread move amongst various types of organisation to gain accreditation for their quality assurance under the British Standard, BS5750/ISO9000. In doing so, these organisations must perceive some potential benefit from possession of the "tick and kite mark" other than just another framed certificate to hang up in Reception. The British Standards Institute lists a number of benefits of having an accredited quality system:

- Improved service performance and customer satisfaction
- Improved productivity, efficiency and cost reduction
- Improved market share

To these may be added other benefits, such as:

- Use as marketing tool
- Access to "preferred provider" lists for contracting
- Increased export markets
- Customers less likely to carry out their own audits, saving time and money
- Reduced quality costs
- Improved company morale

Set against these there are a number of disadvantages to accreditation under BS5750/ISO9000. At the time of writing, a number of critical articles have appeared in certain sections of the press (for example: "How a paper kite is giving nightmares to plumber Tim", *Daily Telegraph*, 15 December 1992; "An MOT for quality? Oh, mercy!", *Daily Telegraph*, 1 February 1993; "Red tape nightmare of BS5750/ISO9000", *Daily Telegraph*, 5 February 1993). These articles, with supporting material and readers' letters, document a number of disadvantages to BS5750/ISO9000:

- High costs of introducing the system, particularly for small companies
- High maintenance costs for retaining accreditation
- The expense of using "quality consultants", whose qualifications, experience of quality systems and suitability are often doubtful
- The impression of blackmail given by large organisations who require BS5750/ISO9000 amongst their suppliers in order to remain on "preferred provider" lists
- The bureaucratic nature of the standard, with its emphasis on documentation
- The difficulty in establishing comparability amongst companies in possession of BS5750/ISO9000, who may vary from large manufacturing concerns employing thousands to one-man service industries. (One of the above articles quotes a one-man grass-cutting service that gained BS5750/ISO9000 to satisfy local authority contractual requirements.)

Whilst many of the above are anecdotal accounts that may be biased, depending on whether the organisation has been successful in gaining accreditation or not, there has been a little research into the experience of companies concerning BS5750/ISO9000. Whittington (1989) examined the interest in, and difficulties of, BS5750/ISO9000 amongst a group of 14 companies in England. Those favouring it gave reasons that stressed instilling discipline in the workforce and retaining customers. Whittington suggested that communication about the standard from the British Standards Institute was seen as vague, with little definition of potential benefits, difficulty in operationalising the standard and those benefits and a resulting lack of perception of benefits. A recent survey by Rayner and Porter (1991) examined the experience of 20 small and medium-sized firms from the heavy engineering and manufacturing industry sectors that had BS5750/ISO9000 accreditation. Using a structured interview, they surveyed a number of variables concerning the implementation of BS5750/ISO9000, and its benefits, costs and disadvantages. The findings of the first study were:

1. Only seven firms attempted to monitor quality costs, and the results from these were judged as inaccurate. Most estimated that failure costs had dropped by a mean of 1.78% of turnover. One of the seven firms reported that failure costs had risen, mainly because of the adoption of more stringent failure criteria.

2. There were a number of reasons for seeking BS5750/ISO9000 accreditation, including customer pressure, the desire to gain new markets and increase market share. Interestingly, only 10% of the firms gave improved product quality as the principal reason for gaining BS5750/ISO9000—80% were more concerned with marketing issues.

3. Of the benefits reported, most of these (40%) were in the area of customer retention, whilst 20% gave gaining new customers as the principal benefit. Other benefits reported included entry into new markets, fewer dissatisfied customers, greater control of business, better internal discipline and reduced scrap and wastage. Of the firms surveyed 75% thought that product quality had improved as a result of installing the quality system. When asked to classify the benefits in terms of two categories, general quality assurance procedure operation and possession

of BS5750/ISO9000, the results were evenly balanced. All marketing benefits were judged to be in the last category, and all the non-marketing benefits were in the former. Most (55%) of the firms felt that the value of the benefits had been in line with expectations, whilst 30% reported them greater than expected.

4. The average time taken to achieve certification was a year, with a range of 4 to 32 months. Costs were divided into two categories: internal (time and effort to install the system) and external (costs of assessment, etc.). The effort in time required ranged from 2 to 500 man-days, with a mean of 179. External costs ranged from £500 to £14 000, with a mean of £5000. Maintenance of accreditation was estimated to cost between £300 and £3000 per annum. A large proportion of firms thought that the costs were greater than expected, but most thought that the benefits outweighed the costs.

5. The greatest difficulty encountered in implementing BS5750/ISO9000 was the lack of management time.

6. Satisfaction ratings were carried out on the subject of third party assessors. Most firms were satisfied with the assessors in terms of promptness, efficiency, professionalism and suitability to the industry in question.

In general, Rayner and Porter conclude that the main benefits of BS5750/ISO9000 were to be gained in the area of marketing, either retaining existing customers or gaining new ones. The costs were high, and a cost-benefit analysis by the authors suggests that there would be considerable cost saving within two years, and the system would pay for itself in the third year after accreditation. The quality system is therefore a medium- to long-term investment. What is unclear is whether these savings result from an effective quality assurance system or from possession of BS5750/ISO9000 per se; the conclusion reached is that without the goal of BS5750/ISO9000, few firms would complete and persist with the installation of such an effective system. Further issues include the question of whether there is compatibility between different organisations with BS5750/ISO9000 who may have very different quality systems and requirements. For example a 95-person engineering organisation might take 32 months implementing the system, requiring a 400-page quality manual, whilst the same standard is reached by a two-person timber yard, with a 400-word manual. What is in question here is the commitment to quality on the part of the organisation, and how much BS5750/ISO9000 reflects this, or is just a process undertaken to meet customer requirements or contractual obligations.

Both the anecdotal reports mentioned above and what little research there is on BS5750/ISO9000 point to some identifiable benefits in terms of marketing and image as well as effects on workforce morale and quality awareness. The improvement of the product is a secondary consideration. Disadvantages include cost, the bureaucratic nature of the system and dissatisfaction with the external assessment system. In the end, each organisation will have to perform its own cost-benefit analysis of BS5750/ISO9000, and weigh up the advantages to it as an independent concern. It is interesting to note that some companies, having done this, opt not to seek accreditation. These companies include some of those seen as paragons of quality products, such as Nissan. Others adopt their own quality system standards which, as in the case of the Ford Motor Company's Q101 standards, are considered more stringent and detailed than BS5750/ISO9000. When, later, we consider the impact of BS5750/ISO9000 on human services, particularly health and social care, these considerations become even more important.

TOTAL QUALITY MANAGEMENT

Earlier in the chapter we saw that there are a number of specific tools and techniques that can be used as part of a general approach to quality assurance in an organisation. In the last section we examined in detail a framework within which quality assurance mechanisms could be placed and evaluated. In the last part of this chapter we will look at the management philosophy that underlies an organisation-wide implementation of both these elements: tools and techniques and frameworks of quality assurance. This is known loosely as "total quality management" (TQM).

Defining TQM

As we have seen, all discussions of quality and quality assurance processes involved detailed discussion of definitions, and each attempt to discuss definitions poses particular difficulty. This is equally true of attempting a definition of TQM. Some writers, particularly the Japanese ones, prefer not to use the term, describing the same concepts as "company-wide quality control" or "total quality control". One of the standard texts on TQM is that by Oakland (1989), from which we have already quoted and cited extensively. He defines TQM as:

> an approach to improving the effectiveness and flexibility of businesses as a whole. It is essentially a way of organising and involving the whole organisation; every department, every activity, every single person at every level. For an organisation to be truly effective, each part of it must work properly together, recognising that every person and every activity affects, and is in turn affected by, others. TQM is a method for ridding people's lives of wasted effort by involving everyone in the process of improvement; improving the effectiveness of work so that results are achieved in less time. The methods and techniques used in TQM can be applied throughout the organisation ... TQM needs to gain ground rapidly and become a way of life in many organisations. (Oakland, 1989, pp. 14–15)

In a recent paper (Dotchin and Oakland, 1992), Oakland has extended this definition by an analysis of the characteristics of total quality as advocated by seven writers, including Juran and Ishikawa. He outlines six features of TQM:

1. TQM is holistic—it concerns the organisation as a whole, with all its functions, employees and suppliers.

2. Customer orientation—TQM is involved with being responsive to customer requirements.

3. Empowering people to achieve quality—TQM stresses the use of management and decision-making techniques that involve all the workforce.

4. Attention to the process—TQM involves detailed attention to the process of service delivery, including the setting of standards and using the tools and techniques of quality control.

5. Quality systems—TQM requires a systematic approach that might be in the form of a framework—such as BS5750/ISO9000.

6. Continuous improvement—TQM stresses a programme and a philosophy of a cycle of continuing quality improvement.

Besides this definition there are few others, and certainly no standard way of defining TQM. As Dale and Plunkett (1991) point out, there are a number of features of TQM that are common to all attempts to define it, and may in themselves serve as a definition. These commonalities are:

1. TQM is an organisation-wide philosophy of management, based on the assumptions of the importance of customer needs and the need for quality processed on the part of the provider.

2. TQM assumes that *everyone* in the organisation is continually involved in improving the elements of the product manufacturing or service delivery processes for which they are responsible.

3. Each person in the organisation is committed to providing the highest level of satisfaction for all their customers, whether they are internal or external.

4. The essence of such improvement is teamwork and collective involvement and improvement, as well as demonstrated commitment by all levels of staff to furthering quality within the organisation.

5. Such participation in the development of quality is recognised and rewarded.

6. Customers and suppliers are seen as an integral part of the quality management process, and their views are sought and valued.

7. Quality improvement is seen as the responsibility of all staff, and is not a function delegated to specialist department, manager or team.

Dale, Lascelles and Plunkett (1990) see TQM as the last stage in the evolution of quality management procedures, whilst at the same time subsuming all the other preceding types. It can be seen as an all-embracing framework within which all aspects of quality are considered.

Tom Peters is acknowledged as one of the "gurus" of management referred to in an earlier chapter. His early work focused on the production of a set of characteristics of what he termed "excellent" companies. He returned to this theme in a later work (1987), and set out 12 characteristics of new companies that have started a "quality revolution". These are:

1. Management is obsessed with quality. This is communicated through concern with the emotional aspects of quality as much as with the practicalities. Quality is at the top of every agenda, and is communicated in symbolic ways through the company. There is persistence in this approach through setbacks, and it is pursued through constant action to improve quality.

2. There is a guiding system or philosophy. Peters suggests that you pick a system and stick with it, as long as it is thorough and rigorously applied.

3. Quality is measured, through, for example, quality costs. The results of the measurement are displayed and communicated, and every worker is involved in the measurement process.

4. Quality is rewarded.

5. Everyone is trained in technologies for assessing quality.

6. Teams involving multiple functions/systems are used. Quality improvement opportunities lie outside the natural work group.

7. Small is very beautiful. Any improvement, however small, is worthwhile.

8. There is constant stimulation.

9. There is a parallel organisation structure devoted to quality improvement.

10. Everyone plays: suppliers, distributors and customers, all must be a part of the organisation's quality process. Likewise all parts of the company must be involved in the quality programme.

11. When quality goes up, costs go down.

12. Quality improvement is a never-ending journey. There must be continual improvement in all aspects of the system.

The Essential Aspects of TQM—Attitudes and Values

Earlier we cited the work of Dale, Lascelles and Plunkett (1990) that suggested that there was a move from more tangible, quantitative methods of quality assurance, with an emphasis on inspection, control and statistical techniques, to methods that stress the inter- and intrapersonal aspects of quality assurance. Above we have reviewed some techniques of quality management, and seen that a similar progression is observable, whilst at the same time placing some of the more analytic techniques in their place in a general framework of quality improvement. Some authors, notably Oakland (1989), Dale and Cooper (1992) and Bright and Cooper (1993) see these aspects as two vital elements in any description of TQM. On the one hand there are the "hard" aspects, including the tools and techniques and the systems or frameworks with which they are employed, and on the other the "soft" aspects, which concern attitudes, values and interpersonal behaviour. Oakland (1989) emphasised that TQM is more concerned with the latter than with the former, although the former have their place as methodological variables. He writes:

> TQM is concerned with moving the focus of control from outside the individual to within; the objective being to make everyone accountable for their own performance, and to get them committed to attaining quality in a highly motivated fashion ... TQM is concerned chiefly with changing attitudes and skills. (Oakland, 1989, p. 26)

Oakland also warns against the danger of preoccupation with the "hard" aspects, which are relatively easier to learn, employ and control, to the detriment of the "soft" aspects. The history of quality in most Western countries shows just such a preoccupation with "magic" techniques, including statistical process control, quality circles and BS5750/ISO9000. Unfortunately, TQM can also be seen in the same light, as some sort of universal panacea for quality problems, or even for organisational problems in general. Heller (1993) stresses this point, and argues that TQM has been seen as just another objective technique of quality, rather than an all-embracing philosophy that is "fundamentally subjective". He suggests that in TQM, all three initials must hold equal weight—it should be total—involving the whole company; quality—in its focus; and about the management of quality.

The essential element of TQM, therefore, is its emphasis on the involvement of the individual's values and attitudes in the development of a quality product or service, and the use of a set of techniques as a framework within which these attitudes and values can be articulated. Some writers, including Cormack (1992) consider that TQM is in itself a set of values, not a set of skills, and suggest that in using TQM an organisation has to consider the processes of value development and attitude change, as well as methods of developing the organisation in such a way that the inculcation of attitudes and values includes the production and commitment to an organisational culture that stresses quality. Bright and Cooper (1993) point out that whilst this is important in manufacturing industry, it is essential in service industries, because of the nature of such industries and their relationship to their customer, as well as the intangibility of the product. In essence, TQM in service industries therefore stresses the internalisation of new values and attitudes, which in itself can change the nature of employee–employer relationships, as Collard (1989) has shown. Bright and Cooper further suggest that using some of the "hard" techniques within TQM leads to some cultural change, and that the major assumption of TQM is that the organisational culture can be managed. They conclude that there is little evidence for the influence of TQM at this deeper level, whilst there is much evidence for organisational change at a superficial level as a result of TQM.

Towards a Framework for Total Quality—Two Models

One of the major aspects of TQM is that it provides a framework for considering all the aspects of an organisation that are concerned with quality, including the "hard" and "soft" ones. Dotchin and Oakland (1992) have outlined a model of TQM that is based on the "soft" aspects of quality, and on the definition of TQM set out earlier in this chapter. Basing on this, and on the analysis of the writings of the major quality gurus, they firstly establish ten points that need to be considered as a background to their model of TQM:

1. The organisation needs long-term commitment to constant improvement.

2. The philosophy of zero errors/defects must be adopted to change the culture to "right first time".

3. People must be trained to understand the customer–supplier relationships.

4. Do not buy on price alone—look at the total cost.

5. Recognise that improvement of the system has to be managed.

6. Adopt modern methods of supervision and training—eliminate fear.

7. Eliminate barriers between departments by managing the process—improve communication and teamwork.

8. Eliminate:

   (a) goals without methods;

   (b) work standards based only on numbers;

   (c) barriers to pride of workmanship;

   (d) fiction—get facts by using the correct tools.

9. Constantly educate and retrain—develop "experts" and "gurus".

10. Develop a systematic approach to managing the implementation of TQM.

From these ten factors, Dotchin and Oakland identify the "soft" outcomes that form the basis of their model, which is summarised in Figure 2.

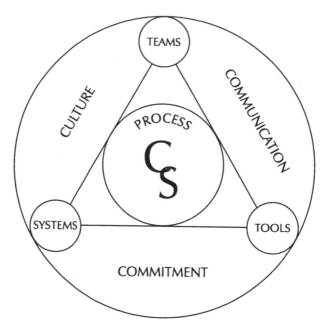

Figure 2   Dotchin and Oakland's TQM model. Reproduced by permission of Carfax Publishing Co. from J.A. Dotchin and J.S. Oakland (1992), Theories and concepts in total quality management. *Total Quality Management*, **3**: 133–145.

In this figure there are five major elements: identifying customer–supplier relationships (C–S in the centre), management
processes, culture, communications and commitment. These "soft"
factors must exist in association with three "hard" management
necessities, systems (based on a good international standard),
teams (such as quality circles, etc.) and tools (such as SPC, etc.).
The authors suggest the application of this three-dimensional
model to examine a particular company's status, or as a guide for
the complete implementation of TQM.

THE QUALITY IMPROVEMENT FRAMEWORK

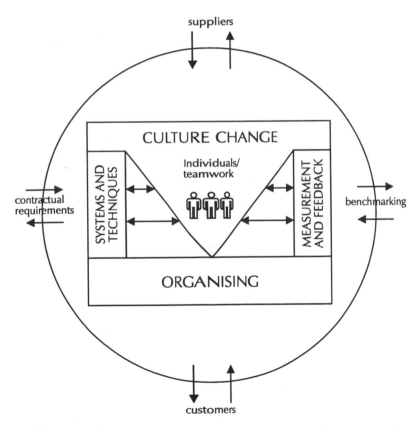

Figure 3 Dale and Boaden's TQM model. Reproduced by permission of
the author's from B.G. Dale and R.J. Boaden (1993), A Total Quality
Framework Which Works, *TQM Magazine*, 5,1, 23–26.

Earlier in the chapter we mentioned a useful framework for considering this type of approach that has been formulated by Dale and Boaden (1993) and described in Boaden and Dale (1993). The reason for producing such a framework was, as with the previous model, the authors' perception that there was a need for an integrative framework, that would draw together the "hard" and "soft" aspects described above, and produce a useful tool for enabling organisations to consider all such aspects when planning or evaluating quality systems. Their "quality improvement framework" appears in Figure 3, and it is used here as an example of a useful way of considering TQM and its processes.

There are four major sections to this model:

1. *Organising*

   This is the foundation stage and is concerned with the motivation for starting a process of quality improvement, and the resulting strategies, plans and policies being adopted. The stage also involves training and the communication of what TQM is about, as well as the identification of potential problems and actions to avoid them. A number of actions comprise this stage:

   (a) A clear long-term strategy for the quality improvement process must be formulated, integrated with other business activities and communicated to all employees. This should also involve the development of quality improvement plans that are more detailed and form objectives against which performance could be judged.

   (b) A common organisational definition of quality and TQM should be arrived at.

   (c) All sources of potential advice and guidance should be identified, and at this stage the consideration of the need for BS5750/ISO9000 should be discussed.

   (d) Formal project planning techniques should be used to identify the necessary stages and actions required to meet the objectives.

   (e) Leadership and involvement should be gained from all management staff, who should see their role as formulating and communicating the "vision of quality and the mission statements that support the process".

(f) A formal programme of education and training should be developed, including "hard" and "soft" aspects of TQM.

(g) An organisational infrastructure that will support, develop, facilitate and maintain the quality approach should be developed and established.

2. *Systems and techniques*

This is the backbone of the quality improvement system, and is concerned with the development of a framework within which quality improvement works, and the application of the "hard" tools and techniques to facilitate this. Actions required include:

(a) Identification of the appropriate tools and techniques, and the processes involved in using them.

(b) Essential training in the use of these tools and techniques.

(c) Consideration of the need for a formal quality system such as BS5750/ISO9000, and if it is decided upon, the necessary requirements should be met.

3. *Measurement and feedback*

This area of the model is where the needs and requirements of the customer or consumer can be translated into measures of performance. Actions required include:

(a) Identifying key internal and external performance measures, and related goals and targets for the improvement set.

(b) Clarifying customer expectations and needs.

(c) Benchmarking against other organisations to ensure best practice.

(d) Deciding on the means for the communication and celebration of success in meeting quality improvement targets, and recognising individual and team efforts.

(e) Linking rewards to quality improvement activities, and ensuring it is a part of all jobs within the organisation.

4. *Changing the culture*

As we have already seen, cultural change is essential for the successful implementation of TQM. Actions in this area include:

(a) Seeing cultural change as a developing entity, and a dynamic one throughout the process of TQM. It will involve planned changes, with an emphasis on communicating the message of quality.

(b) Placing an emphasis on the development of people within the organisation, in skill and personal terms.

(c) Realising the importance of the establishment of teamwork.

(d) Considering the interrelationships of elements within the organisation, to minimise conflict.

(e) Developing performance indicators for the success of TQM on cultural change.

Dale and Boaden outline six stages in the implementation of this model:

1. Reviewing the organisation's adoption of TQM to date.

2. Considering the framework and customising it to suit the organisation and its business.

3. Assessing the features of the organisation against the framework to see which aspects are already in place.

4. Prioritising the features not in place in line with the overall quality strategy of the organisation.

5. Developing plans to introduce the priority features.

6. Identifying potential problems and solutions to them.

In using this framework with a number of organisations and services, the authors recognise and document some of the outcomes. These include its usefulness in general terms as an organising framework, its usefulness as a means of communicating and developing the language of quality, its use as an integrating approach for multisite businesses, and its use as a framework for the audit of TQM implementation.

Implementing TQM and Reasons for its Failure

Despite claims made for its success in changing company performance, there is little documented evidence of the superiority of

TQM over other quality assurance methods. There is also a grow-ing body of literature on TQM failures. Walker (1992), in a review of the literature on this, suggests five reasons why TQM systems fail or underachieve:

1. The efforts involve a great deal of motivational "hype", but do not dedicate sufficient resources for day-to-day running of the system.

2. In manufacturing industries, the main focus is too often the pro-duction unit, to the detriment and neglect of service and mar-keting sides.

3. The TQM system has only limited objectives and defines quality improvement in a restricted way.

4. Organisations view one method—particularly quality circles—as the sole solution to quality problems.

5. The organisations think that simply redoubling existing efforts at quality assurance is sufficient.

By contrast, the successful programmes are characterised by:

1. An emphasis on educating employees in quality and the practi-calities of the business.

2. Inspiration of the employees by leadership and good communi-cation.

3. Participation of employees in quality goal setting and the for-mulation of strategies to meet these goals.

4. Meaningful rewards for success.

5. A focus on the total organisation's effectiveness through the use of cross-functional teams.

Fenwick (1991) suggests that the start-up phase of TQM is the most important, and he offers five (again!) "lessons" in the mechanics of implementing TQM:

1. Choose a start-up strategy based on the company culture, the current quality and business practices, the style of the organisa-tion and the potential impact of TQM implementation on struc-ture and people.

2. Create a vision for the future and determine how TQM will be an integral part of it.

3. Understand that implementing TQM will not be easy, that it will be time-consuming and that it requires personal commitment.

4. Establish benchmarks, which are measurements of the products, services and practices.

5. Network with others involved in TQM.

CONCLUSION

In this chapter we have considered the main features of quality assurance in industry and have examined the basic elements that such approaches require. The need to use objective tools and techniques, within a framework of quality improvement such as BS5750/ISO9000, and with regard to both "hard" and "soft" features of the process, is apparent. The model of TQM presented is one such way of integrating the disparate parts of an overall approach to quality. We will consider in the next chapters the ways in which systems of quality assurance have been applied in human services, particularly health care, and then will examine how such approaches could be used in the therapeutic professions.

CHAPTER 5 Tools and techniques of human service quality 1: Statistical approaches, monitoring and audit

INTRODUCTION

One of the fascinating things about quality assurance in human services is the degree to which they have evolved, and continue to function, without reference to the general models and concepts of quality assurance that we have reviewed in the last chapter. One of the reasons for this might be the widespread view that human services are essentially different to other service industries, and therefore the techniques of quality assurance developed in those industries are inapplicable. As we discussed in Chapters 1 and 2, that is not the view of the present author. Human services are characterised as being high interpersonal contact services, and low tangible product. What is also fascinating is how many of the definitions, concepts and techniques of quality assurance in human services developed in this rather isolated way parallel similar definitions, concepts and techniques found in an examination of the service industry quality assurance literature. In this and the succeeding chapters these parallels will become apparent, and the usefulness of this view of human service quality assurance developed further. We will focus here on the tools and techniques of quality assurance. The examples will be drawn from a wide range of human services, but there will be a bias towards health services, within which unique concepts of quality assurance are well developed, and where the importance of establishing integrated systems is accepted.

In discussing the literature on quality assurance in human services, Dickens (1990, 1991) draws attention to three strands or underlying factors that affect the type of approach taken, and perhaps also explain the reason for the divergence of human service quality assurance mechanisms from those in other service industries. The first strand, which we discussed in Chapter 2 when considering the essential features of human services, is the desire of government or service funders to exercise control, financial, legal or managerial, over what are usually public-funded services. This expresses itself in a number of ways in the establishment of quality assurance mechanisms in such services, including the establishment of legally empowered inspectorates (e.g. the Mental Welfare Commission in Scotland), the creation of advice and consultancy services with an inspection remit (e.g. the Health Advisory Service in the English NHS, and the new "arms-length" inspection units in social services), and the establishment of accreditation schemes and the agencies to carry them out (e.g. the Accreditation Council for Developmental Disabilities in the United States). A second strand is the closer link to academia that is apparent in human services. This leads to an approach to quality assurance that involves research and evaluation, with many "one-off" projects to examine the quality of a particular human service or service component. There are many examples of such approaches and that of King, Raynes and Tizard (1971) is a good early example. These authors attempted to develop objective measures of the quality of care given to children with mental handicaps in residential settings, and then apply them to discriminate between poor and high quality settings and investigate the manipulable dimensions of quality of care as a means to establish better care patterns. The last strand is one which is relatively unique to human services, and that is the one of humanitarian concern. Over the years many attempts to quantify, investigate and develop quality services have come about through the concern of ordinary people with the conditions in, and effects of, human services, particularly where these involve a residential component. This has been expressed in exposés, government and legal enquiries and litigation on behalf of the people served by the service. Residential care for people with learning disabilities in institutions has been transformed in the United States by a number of widely publicised court decisions, where the quality of care and the quality of environment provided by the institutions were made the subject of complaint by people receiving the service, or those acting as advocates and friends. The influence of philosophies and values is strong in motivating and giving expression to this humanitarian concern, and stresses the importance of such considerations when discussing quality in human services, whilst the issue of "quality of life" is an important dimension that might not be addressed in service industries with a lower "human content". We will return to some of these considerations during the course of the next few chapters in our discussions of the tools and techniques of quality.

In the last chapter we also discussed the methods of quality assurance, particularly those tools and techniques that constitute the basic elements of any quality assurance or control system. We saw that these tools varied along a continuum of degrees of "hardness" from the statistical, objective Taguchi techniques with their emphasis on experimental design and control, to quality circles with their stress on the interpersonal processes surrounding quality improvement. In this section of the book we will take a slightly different approach and categorise the tools and techniques not according to this continuum, but according to a number of categories into which the various methods fall. These categories reflect the continuum, however, and it will be seen that some of the techniques mentioned could be considered as an application of their counterparts in the general quality assurance field. As we have again already seen, this similarity is often coincidental, rather than being a determined attempt to use the tools and techniques of industrial quality assurance in the human service environment. The four categories we will consider in the next chapters are: statistical approaches, monitoring and audit; inspection and accreditation; evaluation and research; assessing consumer views.

STATISTICAL APPROACHES, MONITORING AND AUDIT

In earlier chapters we discussed the evolution of quality techniques from early stages that attempted through the use of predominantly statistical techniques to predict and control the production process, to later stages that stressed the organisational and interpersonal context of quality. In the field of human services there has been a similar evolution, although some agencies and services have become preoccupied with certain elements of the continuum to the detriment of others. The three techniques we will discuss here, those of performance indicators, standard setting and monitoring and what is termed clinical audit, reflect on the one hand a desire to obtain the same simple, controllable measures of quality that are apparent in manufacturing industry, and on the other hand show an over-simplification of the complex nature of quality in service industries in general, and human services in particular.

Performance Indicators

Performance indicators (PIs) represent an approach to quality assurance that suggests that quality can be reduced to a set of collectable, measurable, indices of performance, and that human services can therefore be compared in terms of performance on the basis of these indicators. They also are seen as having a utility as standards of quality to be attained by a service, and can be used as fiscal and managerial targets. PIs, in order to be useful, need to be accurate and reliable in terms of the integrity of the data they describe, as well as valid in terms of the meaningfulness of the items measured. For example, for a PI concerning the numbers of clinical psychologists per head of population to be an effective quality measure, we need to be sure that the figures returned from Departments of Clinical Psychology on their staffing levels are reliable and replicable, and that they have been collected in a standard way according to established definitions. We also need to know that there is a causal link between this aspect of clinical psychology and, say, the process or outcome of treatment of patients, for the PI to be valid. That is, more psychologists equal more patients treated and cured. Such validity links are often not established in fact, but are assumed, and it often appears that PIs are chosen because they can be measured and quantified, rather than because they have any validity or predictive power.

PIs are commonplace in most human services, including education and social services, and in some they have reached advanced states of usage. One such example is the use of PIs, termed "Health Service Indicators" in the British Health Service. These date from the early 1980s, when there was a widespread concern within public services in Great Britain to relate performance in such services to expenditure and value for money. The idea of monitoring key indicators of health performance was suggested by the Public Accounts Committee, and a Department of Health and Social Security circular (DA(82)34, 1982) set out the details of the initial system. Central to this initiative was the adoption of a standard method of data collection in the English (not Scottish) Health Districts and Authorities, based on the recommendations of the Körner Committee on health services information. In 1989 a government pamphlet (Day, 1989) stated:

> Health Service Indicators are unique: They comprise the only ready means of making quantitative comparisons between health districts ... The scope of indicators for the NHS was greatly increased in the early 1980s ... so that since 1985 there have been well over 2000 aspects of a (Health) District's services which can be put into the context of all the other Districts in England (and in some cases, Wales and Northern Ireland as well). The indicators are particularly good at two things:
>
> • Providing an overview of a service and thereby pointing towards ways of altering it for the better.
>
> • Giving insights into problems and helping to solve them. (Day, 1989, pp. 1–2)

The data inputs for the PIs used in health services are usually of measurable components of service, such as bed occupancy rates, health professionals per head of local population or number of hospital beds, length of treatment or hospital stay, waiting list length per specialty, and outpatient workload; alternatively they may comprise health-related indices, such as mortality rates, live birth rates and the incidence of specific health problems or diseases. Fenton-Lewis and Modle (1982) suggest that a useful way of classifying PIs in health relates to a model of health-related activities that can be shown as:

$$\text{input} \rightarrow \text{activity} \rightarrow \text{output}$$

where input relates to the resources that produce the planned activity, activity refers to the actions of health professionals (diagnosis, treatment, etc.), and output describes the result of the process in terms of what can be causally attributed to it. This is distinct from outcome, which is defined by the authors as the total change seen in a patient that appears to have some causal link with the activity, but where this link is either partial or assumed. Given this model, Fenton-Lewis and Modle suggest two levels of PIs, Stage 1 PIs that compare the relative efficiency of two or more activities in terms of a ratio of activity to input: this is *efficiency*. Stage 2 PIs compare activity to output, which is *effectiveness*. It can be seen that certain activities may well be efficient, but not effective, whilst the converse may also be true. A quality health activity would attempt to reach both criteria.

Not surprisingly, there have been a number of criticisms of PIs as a measure of quality in health service provision. Many (e.g. Whates, Birzgalis and Irving, 1982) question the accuracy and reliability of the source data, without which the PIs are useless. Others question the relationship between the three elements outlined above. Mullen (1985), reviewing the PIs used in the NHS before 1987, reports that of 135 PIs examined, 43% measured efficiency variables, 11% measured economy of input, 5% measured effectiveness, 1% measured quality, and none measured consumer satisfaction. Of the remaining 40%, most were concerned with "internal balance" or the relationship between services and needs. Mullen also criticises PIs on the grounds that the regular use of indicators tends to modify the behaviour of those in the system subject to these indicators so that the letter of the indicator is met, rather than the overall performance of the organisation being improved. Managers pursue the indicators, not the objectives behind them. She also suggests that indicators serve to stifle initiative and prevent innovation, as improvements may be seen to affect performance on the PIs. PIs can also lead to internal disagreements in an organisation, where the performance of one part of it adversely affects the ratings of another on the PI. Lastly, Mullen suggests there is a need for the development of both "hard" and "soft" indicators, where the former deal in systemic issues, the latter in the interpersonal aspects.

Despite these criticisms, PIs continue to be a road down which many governments travel, and are a reality for many human services. Occasionally the use of PIs leads to important conclusions and valid suggestions for service change. A good example of this is the work of David Braddock in services for developmentally disabled people in the United States (Braddock and Mitchell, 1992), where his costs and staffing comparisons based on a number of PIs show the diversity of services to this client group, raise issues concerning the adequacy of funding and ask fundamental questions concerning staffing and staff turnover.

Standard Setting and Monitoring

The use of performance indicators implies that the performance of a human service system can be quantified and measured in quasi-objective terms, and that, on the basis of these measurements, it can be compared to a similar service to judge comparative performance. A different approach to this is where the service is judged against itself, by the setting of objective targets or standards of performance which can be made the subject of measurement and monitoring, and is assessed according to whether the criteria set in these standards are met or not. This is a commonplace approach in many quality assurance systems used in human services, and is becoming more popular, particularly in Britain, where public services are subject to the standards set out in broad terms in the "Citizens' Charter" and in more specific terms in documents relating to sections of the public service—for example the "Patients' Charter" or the "Parents' Charter". These national documents are accompanied by local level initiatives, and each health provider and education authority has its own version with local targets. As we will see later in this chapter where we discuss quality assurance systems in their totality, standard setting and monitoring is at the heart of most such systems, and is, of course, the basis of BS5750. Most such systems operate on the basis of a quality assurance cycle, and one essential element of this is the selection and definition of standards. A major factor in the use of standard setting approaches is the possibilities they open up for the contractual specification of service quality, one of the main reasons behind their use in many public services (Ashbaugh, 1990). Standards also enable the translation of policies into actions, and the source material from which they are derived will often be legal requirements (such as the Health and Safety at Work Act), government directives or local policies and procedures. Others may come from professional good practice, research and statements of values and philosophies.

To many of the readers of this book the idea of standards as objective statement of performance will not be unusual, as many psychologists, particularly those with a behavioural slant, will be used to writing behavioural objectives that specify performances required of a client in concrete terms. Standards are simply specific expectations of staff performance, described in terms of an activity or outcome against which the performance can be measured. Accompanying a standard will be an indicator or criterion to be achieved in order to measure that performance. One of the main issues concerning the setting of a standard in human services is the level of abstraction that applies to each standard. Many of the performances required of staff are abstract and difficult to measure—for example "staff will treat patients with dignity and respect"—whilst others are more simple and tangible—"residents in the lounge will be observed by care staff three times an hour". Because of the difficulties this poses, many writers talk of the intangibles in terms of "quality statements" or "expectations", and the performances in terms of criteria, which are measurable. (See for example Wilson, 1987, and below.) In any human service it is inevitable that there will be some standards that are more objective than others for the same service. In order for any quality assurance system to be functional and to produce change in the quality of service offered, the standards set, whatever they are called, need to conform to a number of criteria, including:

- *Behavioural*—the standards need to be expressed in terms that specify clearly the performance required, so that there is no dubiety concerning what is being asked of staff. The description should be explicit and precise.

- *Measurable*—the standards need to be definable in terms of a level of performance to be achieved.

- *Understandable*—the standards should be able to be understood by all staff, so the method of expression is important. They should also be logically sound, so that there are no conflicting standards that will cause confusion.

- *Justifiable*—the standards should be acceptable to staff and management, and be seen to be an important element in the provision of a quality service.

- *Realistic*—the standards need to be achievable, and to relate to a realistic view of what can be achieved in performance terms, particularly regarding resource use.

Standards may also be absolute, that is unchanging and universal to that system, or relative, that is related to the specific aspects of the service to which they apply. Reduced to their basics, standards should conform to the same criteria as behavioural objectives, that is they should say *who will do what to what level in which situation*.

A useful model for the process of standard setting and monitoring is contained in the "Manager's Guide to Program Evaluation" published by the Accreditation Council on Services for People with Developmental Disabilities in the United States (ACDD, 1988). This sets out a number of steps to be followed in the process of specifying internal standards for the service, that is the internal measures of performance specific to that agency, as opposed to the external standards that a body such as the ACDD may require for the process of accreditation (q.v. below). These steps, in the form of questions the agency should ask itself, are:

1. What are the agency's goals?
2. What are the agency's objectives?
3. How can these objectives be measured?
4. Who do the measures apply to?
5. When are the measures to be applied?
6. How well is the agency expected to perform?

Standards often form the basis for the audit of professional practice, as Øvretveit (1992) has suggested in his discussion of what he terms "professional quality" in health care. In a later chapter we shall discuss the issue and techniques of this type of internal audit function, particularly clinical audit.

Standard setting has become very popular, as said earlier, in health care, particularly in the nursing profession, and there are many texts on the techniques of standard setting for this profession (see Royal College of Nursing, 1981; Sale, 1990). They are often used in tandem with a number of objective indicators of performance. There are three of these that will be mentioned here.

The first is a system of professional audit known as the "Phaneuf audit" after its author (Phaneuf, 1976). This is essentially a retrospective audit of standards of outcome using records and other information to judge performance. The standards or criteria are predetermined, and centre on seven areas of nursing performance and care given, including the application of the physician's instructions; the observation of symptoms and reactions; the supervision of patients; the supervision of those participating in care; reporting and recording procedures; application and execution of nursing techniques; promotion of physical and emotional health by teaching. Phaneuf developed 50 components from these seven categories to enable assessors to structure the audit of quality, each of which is stated in the form of a performance standard and an observable or recordable criterion. Most of these 50 components are rated on a three-point scale to indicate success or the lack of it.

The second system of standard setting and monitoring is called the Quality Patient Care Scale (QUALPACS) (Wandelt and Ager, 1974), and focuses on the direct and indirect interaction processes between nurse and patient. It contains 68 items divided into a number of scales, including communication, psychosocial aspects (both group and individual) and physical actions. Once again there are explicit statements of the performances required, and the data for the completion of the scale are obtained from observation or from questioning by a nurse trained in the procedure. Each item or standard is rated on a five-point scale, and a total score is obtained.

The third system is known as Monitor, and is an anglicised version of the Rush Medicus system developed in the United States (Goldstone and Illsley, 1986). Based on the idea of definable standards of nursing care, and the quality of it, Monitor assesses four main areas: the planning and assessment of care; the physical and non-physical care delivered; the evaluation of that care; the quality of management of the care process. It consists of a series of checklists relating to specific observable standards. The first of these form the main input, the four divisions of questions. These questions are selected from a master list of some 450 questions on the basis of a dependency classification of the patient in question, and the outcome from the use of Monitor is a percentage score of attainment of standards of performance.

Similar standard setting and monitoring systems exist in other human services. In England the Social Services Inspectorate has produced a number of standards documents for the social care given in various settings to different client groups. In "Homes Are for Living In" (Department of Health Social Services Inspectorate, 1989), a model for evaluating the quality of residential care provided to, and the quality of life experienced by, elderly people in residential care homes is set out. This is based on a number of "principles of residential care", namely privacy, dignity, independence, choice, rights and fulfilment, upon which definitive statements of expectation (similar to standards) are constructed. The scheme then gives a model that can be used for the evaluation of such care settings against these standards.

The use of standards as a method of assuring quality has a number of attractions. Firstly, it is seen to be objective, as the standards contain observable, explicit statements of performances required. As such it comes close to the statistical methods used in manufacturing industry and in other service industries, and enables measurement through observation of specified service delivery processes. Secondly, the process of standard setting itself is a valuable exercise in clarifying values and philosophies, and enables the review of professional practice. Thirdly, standards have multiple use, including the monitoring of performance, the improvement of the quality of the service, the communication of expectations and the setting of management objectives and service performance targets.

Disadvantages to this approach include the difficulty of specifying some of the more "soft" aspects of quality in human services, including the intangibles of interpersonal processes and personality variables that affect performance. Standards may also become expectancies or norms in themselves, with the service performing to standards, rather than trying to improve the service by always increasing the level of performance provided. This is a particular danger where standards are specified in contracts with funding agencies. Standards may also serve to ossify levels of performance that should be dynamic and changing, by perpetuating professional practice through tradition. Mansell (1986) discusses a number of problems in standard-based approaches to quality assurance, including the fact that most systems tend to be biased towards easily-set standards, usually for physical aspects of the service, to the detriment of a wide coverage of all important aspects of quality. He also raises the issue of staff responding more to management needs, that is the achievement of standards of performance, than to the needs of the clients they serve. He criticises the "spurious scientific methodology" that reduces quality to simplistic statistical factors, and ignores the issue of values and attitudes. Lastly, he states that monitoring performance against standards becomes a problem if the standards are irrelevant, or seen to be irrelevant by staff. If so they will not distinguish good performance from bad, but merely register the presence of performance.

Williamson (1992) distinguishes between professional and consumer standards. Both of these are merely qualitative or quantitative expressions of values and philosophies. A consumer standard is one that promotes the interests of the consumer, as defined by the consumer, whilst a professional standard is one which promotes the interest of the consumer, as defined by the professional. These two types of standard are in a state of tension. Sometimes they agree, but often there is disagreement because of a number of factors that Williamson outlines. These include differences in focus of interest, in political and managerial power, and in philosophical position. Whilst both sides wish to see a gradual improvement in standards, there is tension over whether the standards should be detailed or vague. Consumers may wish detailed standards to ensure ease of adherence, whilst professionals may want vague standards to protect professional discretion, "clinical freedom" of action and the development of new methods of accomplishing the desired performance. There is tension over the status of the standards, with professionals favouring standards as guidelines within which various options can be pursued, and consumers seeing them as compulsory, as they then become consumers' rights. Lastly, there is a tension over the level at which the standards are set, and professionals and consumers may disagree as to what constitutes an adequate level of service, the former influenced by the availability of resources, the latter by rights and needs.

Both Performance Indicators and standard setting and monitoring approaches are important elements in any quality assurance scheme, and represent ways of coping with human service quality control that are objective and measurable. They also have an important part to play in any quality assurance scheme that involves audit, inspection or accreditation.

Auditing Human Services—the Case of Clinical Audit

Clinical audit is an extension of the principles outlined above to the setting of standards for professional practice, and the measurement of the performance of the service against those standards, mainly within a health care setting. Within many human services, one of the essential aspects—if not *the* essential aspect of the service's performance—is the competence, skills, knowledge and attitudes of the professional staff that deliver that service. This is particularly the case in health care, with the use of what is commonly called clinical audit (also known as "medical audit", see below), where concern over the quality of medical diagnosis and treatment, particularly by insurance companies that fund medical care in the United States, has led to the use of this technique as one of the main elements in health care quality assurance systems.

For a short time my father was employed as an auditor in his organisation. I well remember the negative, investigative and almost punitive attitude that he had to adopt—much against his true nature—to carry out financial audits of his colleagues' work. Those of us who have experienced a visit from auditors even in an NHS setting will have experienced something like the same attitudes from the receiving end. Clinical audit, however, should be the opposite of that, as it is not concerned primarily with fault or discrepancy finding, but with the examination of working practice to improve effectiveness. At the time of writing, the government is laying great stress on clinical audit as one element in quality assurance in the NHS. The White Paper Working for Patients (1989) defined clinical audit as:

> Systematic, critical analysis of the quality of medical care, including the procedures used for diagnosis and treatment, the use of resources and the resulting outcome for the patient.

In our context, the word medical should be interpreted in its widest possible sense, as is generally the case, so that clinical audit refers to the audit of the work of clinicians from a wide range of disciplines. The possibility of multidisciplinary clinical audit has also been raised, making the applicability of the term particularly wide. There are problems with multidisciplinary audit, however, as Øvretveit (1990) has pointed out. He defines clinical audit as one element of what he calls "professional quality" (as distinct from "client quality" and "management quality"). He considers that because of interprofessional rivalries, differing professional cultures and working practices, uniprofessional clinical audit is the only possible pragmatic starting point in the attempt to monitor and develop the quality of professional input in the NHS. Furthermore, Øvretveit gives three reasons for preferring uniprofessional audit:

1. Audit in general is unfamiliar, and threatening to many practitioners. Even within professions considerable differences are apparent amongst practitioners as to what constitutes high quality services—or even good practice.

2. Audit should form part of the management structure and process. Because most services are still structured by profession, the organisational structure of audit should reflect this, if the process is to lead to effective action in improving professional services.

3. Most experience with audit is within each profession. There are very few generic quality systems in human services, and those that do exist show problems in equal implementation or acceptance.

A recent study for the Department of Health carried out by the Health and Health Care Research Unit of the Queen's University of Belfast has attempted the difficult job of developing a common audit framework for the professions of clinical psychology, speech therapy, occupational therapy and physiotherapy (Normand, 1991). The conclusion reached in this study was that a single system of audit across the four professions was not possible, but outlining a common framework within which intraprofessional development could take place was. We will return to a discussion of this framework when we consider quality assurance in clinical psychology. It should be added that in some situations, particularly those services that operate on a multidisciplinary basis, uniprofessional audit would be irrelevant and inappropriate, as in these settings it is often impossible to separate out the unique professional components of the service provided.

Others have proposed similar definitions of clinical or medical audit, with similar wider applicability, such as Marinker (1990):

> Medical audit is the attempt to improve the quality of medical care by measuring the performance of those providing that care, by considering the performance in relation to desired standards, and by improving on this performance. (p. 3)

The commonality of these definitions is echoed in the four key elements of clinical audit proposed by the Standing Committee on Postgraduate Medical Education in 1989:

A Audit should be directed at quality of care.

B Audit should include the setting of standards.

C Audit should compare performance with these standards.

D Audit should lead to beneficial change.

The similarities between these definitions include the inclusion of Donabedian's structure, process and outcome dimensions already mentioned, the idea of setting standards and measuring performance against them, and of a degree of systemisation of the process of audit. Another basic element is the idea of a systematic approach to the process, with documentation, specification, measurement and evaluation of outcomes as essential parts of the procedure. Considerable confusion still exists, however, among clinicians and managers because of the use of the terms "clinical audit", "medical audit" and "quality assurance" to describe the same activity. Harman and Martin (1992) suggest that this is a disagreement not of principles, but of methodologies. They describe how clinicians see audit as a matter of professional development, education and research, while managers see it as a matter of accountability for the use of resources, and of efficiency and effectiveness. The answer to these misunderstandings lies perhaps in the incorporation of clinical audit as one element of a comprehensive quality assurance programme that includes other methods and measures for the examination of non-clinical and managerial aspects of care, and in the crucial role of professionals, including clinical psychologists, in making clinical audit a relevant and important part of the evaluation and monitoring of their clinical practice. In that way clinical audit will provide not only management information on the quality of clinical care, but also material for the improvement of professional standards, topics for future research, and elements of necessary teaching and education.

As with a definition of clinical audit, there are also differing opinions about the process, although again there are similarities in the basic principles and the methodology involved. Russell and Wilson (1992) suggest that there are three essential steps in what they call the audit cycle: set the standard; observe practice and compare with the standard; implement change. Basing it on these three steps they outline a detailed nine-step process model for conducting rigorous scientific clinical audit, which they consider the third clinical science (the other two being exploratory and pragmatic research):

A   Choose a general topic for audit and a specific hypothesis to be tested.

B1 Develop a standard.

B2 Disseminate the standard.

B3 Implement the standard.

C1 Design unbiased and precise methods for sampling patients.

C2 Collect valid and reliable data on performance.

C3 Compare these performance data with the standards by careful statistical analysis.

C4 Feed a clear summary of this comparison back to participants.

D   Ensure that this process generates beneficial change.

Although the above steps were described by the authors in a medical context, using general medical illustrations, the same steps would appear to have an appeal to clinical psychology, with its emphasis on the hypothetico-deductive scientist–practitioner role. The stress placed on validity and reliability and statistical analysis should be a natural one to most psychologists and fits with other aspects of clinical practice such as psychometrics.

Marinker (1990) has a similar set of steps in a seven-stage model of audit that he proposes in the context of medical general practice:

A Determine which aspects of current work are to be considered.

B Describe and measure present performance and trends.

C Develop explicit standards.

D Decide what needs to be changed.

E Negotiate change.

F Mobilise resources for change.

G Review and renew the process.

In contrast to the steps outlined above, this model stresses the organisational aspects of audit as opposed to the scientific process, and points up the need for considering various resource factors such as the information required for decision making and monitoring of performance, the technology necessary to handle this information, the staff available to conduct the process and analysis, the time required of clinicians for audit to be a meaningful activity, and lastly the cost implications along the lines of cost-benefit analysis.

Lastly, Dixon (1989) suggests a similar seven-step approach, involving:

1. Design: select audit subject, specify objectives and select patient group.

2. Decide indicators: decide how patient care is to be measured in relation to audit objectives, and decide on data collection methods.

3. Collect and organise data: comparison of cases against indicators.

4. Analyse data: non-conforming cases are identified and studied.

5. Identity problems and possible causes.

6. Take action: to remedy identified problems and their causes.

7. Follow-up to see if the action taken accomplished the desired outcome and eliminated the problem.

Whatever model or process is followed, the importance of maintaining a systematic, scientific approach, and basing action for improving quality on data and on good practice, remains. A good procedural guide has been outlined by Shaw (1991). Based on these processes, four types of medical audit are usually defined (e.g. see Øvretveit, 1992):

1. *Internal retrospective audit*: this is the most simple to carry out, and as a result is the most commonly used type, particularly in the NHS. In this method a specialty or department will analyse past case records, perhaps selected on a random or sampled basis, and assess them against the set criteria.

2. *External retrospective audit*: this is undertaken by a professional group, in cooperation with an external body, particularly an academic college or professional institution. This also involves the process of peer review, that has been developed by Heron (1979) and Øvretveit (1988).

3. *Concurrent active audit*: this is a review of the care and treatment given to patients whilst they are still within the system and under care. It may involve the use of the type of checklist system mentioned above in the context of standard setting.

4. *Criterion-based audit*: this involves explicit and measurable criteria of good practice, which are then used to assess the performance of professionals on a selected number of cases.

There are many studies reported that show the benefits of using audit techniques in the improvement of the quality of clinical services in the health care field. Most of these are drawn from the acute physical illness files of medicine, and few reports exist concerning the use of clinical audit techniques in services closer to the social care area of human service provision. As a result, clinical audit could be seen to perpetuate a view of quality assurance that sees it as solely the business of the professionals, who not only set the agenda, but also carry out the audit with little reference to consumers. We have already mentioned Williamson's (1992) writings on this topic above. Clinical audit appeals to the medical profession, who see it as a way of appeasing management and consumer demands for accountability, whilst retaining the pseudo-scientific and academic mystique of medical practice. Øvretveit (1992) also criticises the simplistic type of audit that has been promulgated and used in the British health care system, and the non-specific way it has been introduced, as opposed to the mandatory, management-linked systems common in North America. He sees this as posing a credibility problem to professionals, with the acceptance of an informal and unsystematic method, which may result in audit as a whole being discredited. It has also yet to be demonstrated that the cost of audit is justified in terms of saving achieved as a result of the implementation of new practices. This is a pertinent point in view of the increasing linkage of audit to information technology, and the use of computers to aid the process. Packwood (1991) suggests that clinical audit has three activity foci: as a professional activity, an educational activity, and a management activity. At present it has still to be shown that audit is an adequate technique for improving quality in any one of these foci, as it is tool-episodic, unstructured and does not link into management action. Ellis (1988), reviewing the use of medical audit in Britain, reports that the attempts to introduce it to that date had been sporadic, unsystematic, local and disaster-driven.

In conclusion, it can be seen that clinical audit, which is almost exclusively used in health service settings, meets criteria of professional acceptability, but does not incorporate consumers in any meaningful way. It may have a place within a quality assurance system framework as one element in the evaluation and monitoring of professional activity, but it does not, on its own, form an adequate quality control technique.

CHAPTER 6

Tools and techniques of human service quality 2: Inspection, accreditation and service evaluation

THE ROLE OF EXTERNAL AGENCIES

The methods outlined in the previous chapter stressed the *internal* aspects of quality assurance, with the development of standards and measures of performance by the agency itself, and the audit of performance based on mutual review against internally-agreed criteria. Many of these standards may, however, also represent *external* standards of performance, or at least criteria of quality that are applicable across many settings either in the same human service function, or derived from universal principles that guide such services. In most human services, for example, the principle of dignity and respect is evident, both on a general level concerning the values that underlie that service, and on the specific level of the definition of performances or the methods of achieving performances in the service delivery process that will stress respect.

In this section we will review the approach to quality assurance that stresses the role of external agencies in the process, and particularly the inspection and audit function of legal and voluntary bodies in the human service field.

INSPECTING THE SYSTEM AND ITS COMPONENTS

Most human services, because of their dependence on public funds, are subject to inspection as a means of ensuring the efficient use of those funds. Examples can be found in all human services— we have already quoted from a document prepared by the English "Social Services Inspectorate" (q.v.)—and there are many others in England—Her Majesty's Inspector of Constabulary; Her Majesty's Inspector of Schools, to name but two. Similar inspectorates are present in most countries, for example the New York State Commission on Quality of Care for the Mentally Disabled, and the Commission on Corrections. In most cases the bodies set up to undertake such inspecting functions are statutory agencies, mandated and funded by government or public bodies, and are financed by public funds. They may also have statutory duties and legal requirements.

Such inspectorates may also operate on different time scales; some may be set up for the purpose of inspecting or investigating specific services or specific incidents within services. The British Committee of Enquiry system is a good example; these are quasi-legal bodies that are set up to investigate, on a retrospective basis, incidents or conditions that have occurred in a human service, and to report on findings in order to make recommendations that might remedy the problems. An example of such specific inspectorates and their output is the Report of the Committee of Enquiry into Allegations of Ill-Treatment of Patients and Other Irregularities at the Ely Hospital, Cardiff (1969); others concentrate on similar investigations of "scandals" in hospitals, residential care, and most recently, in the handling of child sexual abuse accusations. Whilst these Committees concentrate their efforts on specific services, and often on very limited aspects of those services, the conclusions reached may be used to frame legislation or to define good practice—that is quality—in similar services in general. The Butler-Sloss enquiry into the Cleveland child abuse issue in England, for example, led to the issuing of guidelines for health care and social work professionals on the handling of children suspected of having been abused.

There exist, however, in most countries, longer term inspectorate bodies that carry out similar work on the basis of monitoring rather than investigation. Often these bodies may have been established because of a specific incident, or a series of incidents, within a service that led to the type of inspection/enquiry approach detailed above. An example of such an inspectorate that developed because of the results of public enquiries is the English Health Advisory Service, previously the Hospital Advisory Service. This Service, described more fully in Seager (1991), monitors and inspects services for people with mental illness, elderly people and those with addictions, in England and Wales. Similar inspectorates exist in Scotland and Northern Ireland. As Seager admits, the underlying reason for the establishment of this inspectorate was a series of "scandals" in long-stay institutions, and the resulting political embarrassment for the government of the day. The remit of this inspectorate is to inspect and advise on the state of services for the above client groups, and to be a source of advice for change, in the form of the promulgation of "best practice". When originally established, the Health Advisory Service also monitored services for people with learning disabilities, but this aspect of the work was separated in 1976 with the further establishment of another inspectorate to fulfil the same functions solely for this client group, namely the National Development Team. At the time of this change, the remit of the Health Advisory Service was widened to include community facilities as well as hospitals—hence the change in name.

The Health Advisory Service, in common with many similar bodies, visits services with a multidisciplinary team of professionals, usually for an extended period of two to four weeks, seeing all aspects of each service and meeting significant people within the service, as well as consumers and those with peripheral interests. Most inspectorates follow defined guidelines for structuring their evaluation, but do not use standard instruments of evaluation. The end product is usually a written report to government and to the service and its funding bodies, as well as to other interested agencies. The report not only gives information on the state of the service at the time of the visit, but also carries recommendations for change. The reports of the Health Advisory Service are, however, advisory, and might not always be implemented.

Other countries have similar quasi-legal bodies. In The Netherlands a division of the Public Health Supervisory Service called the Medical Inspectorate of Mental Health monitors and inspects facilities for those with mental illness and learning disability. The visits are conducted in accordance with a "Frame of Reference" (Medical Inspectorate of Mental Health, 1987), which is really a set of standards against which the service will be inspected, using similar techniques to its British equivalent. In the United States, both Federal and State bodies exist to license human services to various client groups, and these bodies may also fulfil the role of an inspectorate, with regular visits to services and reporting on conditions to government. They are very little different from the accreditation schemes that exist in the United States, which we will discuss in the next section.

Lastly, it should be mentioned that there will be an increase in monitoring and inspecting of human services at least in the health and social care field in Great Britain as a result of recent legislation, management structure and organisational changes in the respective bodies. Most local authorities and health boards and authorities now have a contracting and purchasing function, with contracts let to service providers. Part of the system is an extensive contract monitoring system, which will involve these authorities in the regular visiting, inspecting and monitoring of services contracted to them. In many cases quality standards are built into the contracts, and so the inspecting function will focus extensively on the quality of service and care being delivered, as well as on value for money, efficiency and effectiveness. In the case of local authorities, they are charged with the duty of setting up the so-called "arm's length" inspection agencies—that is inspection units that have only a limited relationship with the authority and are semi-independent—to inspect and monitor the quality of services being delivered under contract by service providers, particularly in the residential care setting. Similar duties are carried out by health authorities in respect of the registration of nursing homes and other forms of residential care for various client groups. In most cases model guidelines or standards exist, against which the service is assessed.

The strength of this type of approach to the assurance of quality lies in the application of an external objective review of services, particularly where this is allied to a frame of reference that gives an overview of service provision for a particular client group elsewhere, and a set of defined quality standards against which the service may be judged. A second strength is the legalistic nature of such evaluations, and the weight that can be applied to the outcomes in terms of obtaining implementation. The drawbacks are: the superficiality of the approach, where inspection visits are, logistically, of short duration; the lack of involvement of staff of the service in the process and outcome of the inspection, leading to the setting up of situations purely for the purpose of inspection; and the assessing of the service purely in terms of professionals with a consequent lack of consideration of users' views and the perpetuation of models of service and service practices and processes that suit professionals, not the users. (See Williamson, 1992, for a similar discussion in terms of the setting of standards.)

Accreditation Schemes

A similar approach to quality assurance in human services to the one described in the last section is the use of accreditation systems and agencies to inspect, monitor and register or license facilities or services in a particular specialty. The main difference between the approach mentioned there and accreditation is the fact that licensure and inspection is usually a governmental, administrative-based procedure, which consists of inspection, reporting and granting of a licence to operate (not always, particularly within the British system) as a result of that process. Accreditation on the other hand is a voluntary process, with review by peers. Hemp and Braddock (1990) quote Elizabeth Boggs:

> The role of voluntary nongovernmental bodies is improving standards, securing consensus, and assisting providers to improve their performance ... Public licensure ... responds to the ultimate demand for public accountability. (Hemp and Braddock, 1990, p. 189)

Thus accreditation and licensure should be complementary. Both these authors see accreditation as an essential element of quality assurance in human services. The United States and Canada have the most well-developed system of accreditation in the human services field, with bodies such as the Committee on Accreditation of

Rehabilitation Facilities, The Accreditation Council on Services for People with Developmental Disabilities (ACDD) and the Joint Commission on the Accreditation of Hospitals. All these agencies accredit services: Øvretveit (1992) points out that an important role of accreditation is in the accreditation of people, where professionals are assessed against criteria of professional practice and knowledge, and granted operating status as a result of a positive assessment. In the United States, medics must undergo regular accreditation. In the British NHS, many professionals can only practise if accredited by their professional body. In the profession of clinical psychology, for example, one form of accreditation is the Register of Chartered Psychologists, and the accompanying requirement for an annual practising certificate. Membership of the register is granted following an academic and/or professional review process.

Accreditation in Action—the ACDD

As an example of the type of approach an accreditation service might take to assuring quality in the services it covers, it is worth examining the services offered by the ACDD in the United States. Gardner and Parsons (1990) define this as "an organisation uniquely dedicated to the promotion of quality services for individuals with developmental disabilities" (p. 207). The ACDD fulfils a number of roles in doing so, including assisting agencies to identify, embrace and express the values and expectations of their consumers, providing an external point of reference against which the service may judge its performance and assisting the agency in the process of developing a quality assurance system. There are a number of aspects to its work:

1. The development of standards and guidelines. The ACDD publish a set of standards (ACDD, 1990) which consist of 817 specific standards under the headings: values, the agency, habilitation and support services, and environment. The standards represent a consensus of opinion amongst professionals and lay people who represent consumers about what comprises high quality service. There are two types of standards, those that reflect organisational characteristics or practices, and those that relate directly to individuals within the service. These

standards are periodically revised in the light of new knowledge, technology, experience and concepts.

2. Development of training materials. ACDD publishes a number of guides to service quality assurance and the development of aspects of the organisation.

3. Provision of training, technical assistance and consultancy, in an effort to improve services.

4. Accreditation surveys, using the standards, are carried out by ACDD staff. Self-assessment and site visits are carried out, resulting in an accreditation decision.

ACDD accreditation, whilst voluntary, is often mandated by some states for all facilities, with provision for regular review and reaccreditation. In a survey by Hemp and Braddock (1990), of 186 agencies surveyed between 1983 and 1984 by ACDD, covering large and small public and private residential and non-residential facilities, 70% were granted accreditation.

One aspect of accreditation that is evident in the work of ACDD is the fact that the approach taken is a development one, rather than an objective external inspection one. The ACDD encourages a process of strategic planning, organisational development, programme evaluation and staff orientation and training, and these are seen as significant outcomes by Gardner and Parsons. It influences strategic planning by focusing the attention of the agency on individual clients' needs and futures, and their interaction across programmes in a coordinated way. It encourages organisational development through the process of self-assessment, which in itself requires intra-agency coordination and teamwork. The outcomes for programme monitoring include a realistic view of the benefits of the service to the people it serves, and a review of staffing and the environment within which the service operates, both physical and organisational.

Organisational Audit

In Great Britain the use of accreditation is limited to individual accreditation, or to the accreditation of parts of the system, usually for the purposes of training other professionals. Stocking (1989) argues that there is a need for uniformity of approach into the quality assurance systems in the British NHS, which might be brought about by accreditation and the requirement for this in contracts between purchasers and providers. A systematic attempt to introduce this type of approach has been made by the King's Fund Organisational Audit Programme, set up in 1989, and described in Brooks (1992). This takes the North American accreditation organisations as its model, with the emphasis on a framework of organisational standards for quality and the evaluation of the performance of a health care organisation against these standards by an external voluntary body.

The standards developed by this programme apply mainly to acute illness hospitals, and cover:

- Patient's rights and special needs
- Managerial and support services
- Professional management
- Departmental management

Within each of these sections there are subelements, consisting of:

- Philosophy and objectives
- Management and staffing
- Staff development and education
- Policies and procedures
- Facilities and equipment
- Evaluation and quality assurance

Evaluation against these standards consists of a survey and a self-assessment. The survey team of professionals interviews staff, managers and patients, observes the environment and checks documentation. As with ACDD, the King's Fund programme stresses the need for the accreditation process to be a form of organisational change as well, and so a procedure for the development of the standards and their application in the hospital concerned is laid down. The final result is a comprehensive report, but at present there is no award of accredited status.

Brooks reports a number of benefits from this type of organisational audit:

1. A framework is established for incorporating existing quality assurance procedures and coordinating them.

2. Good practice is validated and recognised in documentation.

3. It provides an opportunity for multidisciplinary review in a systematic way, with a focus on the standards that encourage cooperation rather than competition.

4. Improved communication.

5. The concluding report provides an agenda for future action on quality.

6. It can provide a basis for negotiation between contractors and providers on the ways of monitoring quality.

Despite these benefits, accreditation has a number of drawbacks as a mechanism for quality assurance. Øvretveit draws attention to a number of these, including the doubts concerning the cost-effectiveness of external review, and the difficulties imposed by a proliferation of bodies, each with different standards, as is the case in the United States. He also is uncertain as to the extent to which consumers are involved in the process, which raises the criticism of accreditation merely perpetuating professional self-interest.

Other criticisms of accreditation come from research. Two papers are seminal in this respect, both concerning services for people with learning disabilities. Repp and Barton (1980) observed staff practices and interactions with residents in institutions that had accreditation (and licensure) and those that did not. Their conclusion is:

> The data show that there is little difference and this result has two implications: (a) that various standards and guidelines may not be getting at the heart of the matter ... and (b) that a unit or facility may be licensed even when it is not providing active habilitation. (Repp and Barton, 1980, p. 339)

Similarly, the connection between accreditation and changes and improvements in day-to-day practice is questioned by Bible and Sneed (1976), who observed staff behaviour in an institution for people with learning disability during a visit by an accreditation team and directly after. They found a 256% increase in the duration of staff–resident positive interactions during the visit, with an immediate reversal to the original level once the visit was over! Accreditation cannot, by itself, guarantee that a quality approach is taken at all times. It can give a retrospective "snapshot" view at a given point in time, which may or may not be valid at any other time. By itself it is not an adequate approach to quality assurance in human services.

HUMAN SERVICES EVALUATION

There is a long history of an approach to assessing, monitoring and improving quality in human services based on a quasi-academic, research-orientated approach that is focused on evaluation, and the use of a set of concepts and techniques that owe more to the discipline of the scientist–practitioner than to that of the quality engineer. This approach is very popular in the United States, where there is a flourishing evaluation industry, and from where most of the standard texts on the subject originate. In Britain, evaluation is an activity carried out mainly in an academic context, as operational research.

Defining Evaluation

In a major text on the topic, Rossi and Freeman (1982) define evaluation as:

> The systematic application of social research procedures in assessing the conceptualisation and design, implementation and utility of social intervention programmes. (Rossi and Freeman, 1982, p. 20)

This definition emphasises the vital link between evaluation and research—evaluation is the application of techniques developed in a "pure" research setting to human services and their effect on alleviating human problems. Posavac and Carey (1980) see evaluation as fundamentally to do with providing feedback on social systems, and as such it should not be confused with two related activities: basic research and individual client assessment. The former is the use of the same techniques, but with the emphasis on investigating questions of theoretical interest, and the proving or disproving of hypotheses of a theoretical nature. The latter is a professional activity which focuses on an individual and the assessment of their needs, rather than on an assessment of the system within which the service to meet those needs is delivered.

Coursey (1977) considers that the understanding and definition of evaluation can only be accomplished with a corresponding understanding and definition of the nature of human services—or the "programs" to which almost all evaluation literature relates (and consequently "program" will be retained in the following discussion). He defines a program as follows (Coursey's italics):

> The *staff* engage in certain specified *activities* (e.g. psychotherapy), with certain types of *clients* (drug addicts, school system, etc.), using certain *resources* in order to achieve some specified *goals*. Program activities are based on certain *assumptions* or theories: namely that specified activities effect changes in clients in the expected goal directions. In addition, a program requires certain *support functions* (e.g. resource gathering, coordination, secretarial help, etc.) from the agency in which the program operates. (Coursey, 1977, p. 5)

In this context, therefore, evaluation asks questions of all or any of these components, as well as their interrelationships, and their relationships with the wider systems within which they operate. Coursey continues:

> Program evaluation, then, consists of determining the relative worth of a program, or parts of it, by examining some salient aspects of it. Program evaluation seeks to provide an objective, factual base for making decisions about program improvements, changes or termination. (Coursey, 1977, p. 5)

Evaluation Approaches

Program evaluation is a very new field of applied social science, and derives its concepts and methodologies from a number of sources, including sociological research, psychometrics, anthropological research and epidemiology. Its essence is pragmatics—hence the lack of unifying theoretical consideration amongst the possible definitions of evaluation. Stecher and Davis (1987) write:

there is no single, agreed upon definition for evaluation. Neither is there a single set of acceptable procedures that one follows in carrying out an evaluation study. Instead there are a number of different conceptions about what evaluation means, and how it should be done. (Stecher and Davis, 1987, pp. 22–23)

These authors then set out a number of approaches, based on the assumptions made about evaluation, and how it should be carried out, that form a historical progression in the history of evaluation approaches. This moves from approaches that were closer to pure research, such as using control groups and rigid experimental designs, to a more "humanistic" approach, where interpersonal processes, including those of the program with the evaluator, form part of the process, and in which qualitative measures play as important a part in evaluation as qualitative ones. The five approaches they outline are:

1. *The experimental approach*: this approach is the earliest form of program evaluation, and stresses the application of the principles of experimental design and analysis to human service evaluation. Using controlled experimentation, the evaluator attempts to derive generalisable conclusions about a particular program and its aspects by controlling variables and isolating influences. The attraction of this approach is its objectivity, and its relationship to the scientific method. The intervention is clearly defined. The methods selected are rigorous, and might include the use of matched controls, randomisation or longitudinal analysis. Conclusions are then drawn on the basis of the data and evidence collected and whether this proves or disproves a hypothesis. Because of the rigorous nature of the method, replication and generalisation of the conclusions may be possible. The disadvantages to this approach include the fact that human services cannot be as rigidly controlled as may be possible in an artificial research setting, and the lack of consideration of the interpersonal aspects of the intervention process itself.

2. *The goal-orientated approach*: this is a more pragmatic approach than the experimental one and seeks to clarify further the program's goals and set up an evaluation that assesses the performance of the program against these predetermined goals. The approach has an advantage in that it can help to clarify desired

outcomes for the program, and the activities needed to accomplish them. The measures involved will necessarily revolve around these outcomes, and may include measures of goal attainment such as Goal Attainment Scaling (Kiresuk and Sherman, 1968). The selection of measures will depend to a great extent on the nature of the goals, and whether these are outcome-orientated or process-orientated. Disadvantages of this type of approach are the neglect of other aspects of the program that a narrow focus of goals implies. Campbell, Steenbarger, Smith and Stuckey (1982) suggest that a systems approach to evaluation is better, as it emphasises the interrelationships amongst various components of the program that will have a bearing on the outcomes accomplished.

3. *The decision-focused approach*: this emphasises the systematic collection and analysis of information about the program for the purposes of management decision making and monitoring of performance. The goal of this type of evaluation is therefore to directly effect improvements in the program. Such an approach involves information systems and the specification of data required for decisions to be made. It has the advantages of being directly designed to influence the process of the program. The evaluator is therefore more closely involved in the program than in the first two approaches above. Disadvantages can arise from this closeness, with the loss of objectivity, and the danger that the evaluator is seen merely as a tool of management control.

4. *The user-orientated approach*: this approach stresses the utility of the evaluation, and the evaluator is concerned with maximising the implementation of the findings by the selection of program focus to evaluate and the techniques and methods used to evaluate the program. The user-orientated approach stresses the interpersonal aspects of the evaluation, including the style and sensitivity of the evaluator, considers the organisational and societal context of the program and involves the users of the program directly in the evaluation. The types of methods used will include stakeholders' and program consumers' groups, and a "process consultancy" model (Schein, 1980) may be used. The advantages of this approach include the involvement of users and seeing the program from their perspective, as well as possible increased implementation of the findings because of an ownership of the process by the program. Disadvantages include the

possibility of bias from strong pressure groups concerned with the program, and difficulties in clarifying who the true consumers are.

5. *The responsive approach*: this is a combination of the systems approach alluded to above and the user-orientated approach. The basis of this approach is the evaluation of the program in terms of the multiple perspectives of the people involved with the program, and the differing values, objectives and expectations that arise from this. The approach stresses a methodology that relies heavily on qualitative, individual perceptions, gained through interview and observation of the program process, and specific techniques such as social network analysis and transactional analysis might be employed. The advantages of this type of approach are its ability to cope with complex, changing systems, and multiple viewpoints, but its disadvantages include subjectivity, and the lack of rigorous consideration of outcomes and process variables.

Each of these approaches should be matched to the human service being evaluated, as no claims are made as to the superiority of one approach over another; they are merely different, and will suit different situations. The evaluator must select an approach and methods with care and sensitivity.

Posavac and Carey present an alternative classification of evaluation approaches, which is based on the function and purpose the evaluation is serving. This can be:

1. *The evaluation of need*: an evaluation may well focus on the needs of the community for the program being evaluated, or for programs of a particular type. It is obviously closely linked to service planning and development processes, and will use techniques such as surveys, needs assessment and epidemiological analysis.

2. *The evaluation of process*: this evaluation approach looks at the extent to which a program is implemented as designed and is achieving performance goals. It may include the type of performance indicators we have reviewed above as one of its data inputs, backed up by observation and interview of staff and clients.

3. *The evaluation of outcome*: this is one of the major areas for evaluation studies, and looks at the effectiveness of a program in achieving its stated goals and objectives. It is also fraught with difficulties, not the least of these being an agreed definition of success for the program, and the establishment of causal links between program efforts and client outcomes. The methods involved will be more complex, and might involve comparative studies, using control groups or situations, and standard or devised outcome measures.

4. *The evaluation of efficiency*: evaluation may also focus on the degree to which the program is cost-effective in achieving its goals and objectives. The crucial criteria to be considered centre on effectiveness and cost, and the tools employed may owe more to economics than socio-psychological techniques, with the employment of cost-benefit analysis and other formulae.

The Process of Evaluation

Most evaluation studies, whichever approach they use, follow a pattern of activities as far as implementation is concerned, and this pattern reflects the objective, analytical, scientific approach that is a feature of evaluation as a discipline in general. There are a number of stages in the implementation process that may be defined.

Stage One: Defining the program and its components, and setting the purpose of the evaluation.

The boundaries of the subject of the evaluation need to be decided upon, and the extent to which all components of the program will be involved in the evaluation. This also involves consideration of the systems within which the program operates, and the extent to which they also will be involved in the evaluation. It is a stage at which much negotiation must be undertaken by the evaluator. Sometimes the evaluation is an invited process, whereby the program itself sees the need for an evaluation in order to clarify its purpose and achievements, but often evaluation is a mandatory process, and there may be resistance on the part of program staff to the idea. The clarification of purpose is also a major feature of this stage, and, as we have seen, will have a significant effect on the selection of the most appropriate approach or method by the evaluator. The negotiations required will enable the evaluator to establish his or her identity and credibility with program staff, as well as helping to identify possible sources of information or, alternatively, potential problems. The main questions to be asked at this stage include:

- Who wants the evaluation?

- What do they want from the evaluation?

- Why do they want the evaluation?

- When do they want the evaluation?

- What resources are available for the evaluation?

Additionally at this stage the definition of program goals is important, particularly if the evaluation is to focus on outcome and effectiveness, and these goals need to be agreed between evaluator and program.

Stage Two: Developing an evaluation approach and methodology.

This stage involves an examination of the literature on the type of program being evaluated, and on evaluation in general, in order to guide the selection of the most appropriate methodology for the evaluation. Methodology is a complex area, and an appreciation of the available methods is essential for the matching of program and approach. Coursey (1977) notes three factors in this matching and selection process. Firstly, the evaluator and the program should consider the available resources and capabilities for implementing and sustaining what could be a complex procedure. Secondly, the approach taken, and the experimental design it suggests, should flow from, and be in harmony with, the purpose of the evaluation. Thirdly, when judging the effectiveness or outcome of a program (the most common type of evaluation), two factors should be considered, one the establishment of a basis for comparison (i.e. treatment versus no-treatment, pre- versus post-testing, etc.) and the other the need to have a design that allows for the ruling out of alternative explanations for the changes observed as a result of the program's interventions.

The crucial element in evaluation is the experimental design that will be used, and this is something to be considered at this stage.

Campbell and Stanley (1963) and Cook and Campbell (1979) have outlined a number of experimental designs that can be used. They are particularly concerned with the "threats to validity" that occur in many simple experimental designs, particularly the classic pre-test–post-test design, which limits the interpretability of the data obtained in the light of the way in which the data were collected. These threats include actual but non-program-related changes in the program participants (e.g. children in a program being evaluated will develop and mature, and external events may radically change the participants in a way that impacts on the program); the participants may not be a random or representative sample of the people who might benefit from the program, through biased selection, selective mortality and regression to the mean in terms of the probability of success; there may be instrumental effects because the measures that are being employed are not themselves reliable or valid, and the effects of repeated testing with the same measure will increase performance levels. In order to get around some of these effects, these authors suggest a number of "quasi-experimental" research and evaluation designs. These designs, whilst not achieving the level of control of variability of true "pure" experimental situations, are suited to evaluations because they control for many sources of bias, and can therefore yield interpretable results. The bases of the methods are the observance of program participants at additional times, both before and after the evaluation period, observing additional people who have not received the program, and using a variety of variables, some of which will be expected to be influenced by the program, and some not. Examples of the specific techniques suggested are time-series analysis, which looks at information and change in the information over a number of time intervals, and non-equivalent control group design, using comparison groups of similar subjects to the program participants, in order to judge the magnitude of the change in the latter group. Other important experimental designs include the use of randomised controlled trials (fully described in Boruch and Rindskopf, 1984), which are heavily used in health care service evaluation, particularly in the acute medicine field, and involving the comparison of various types of drug treatment. Randomised controlled trials assign participating clients randomly to an experimental (treatment) or control (no treatment) group, often using "double-blind" methodology to ensure that the evaluator or program worker is not aware to which group the client is assigned. They are particularly valuable in evaluating effectiveness, but have been suggested to have little value in the evaluation of human services that focus on multiple factors or are delivered in a multidisciplinary setting. They are also unsuitable for settings that do not permit the experimental manipulation of treatment conditions, which is often the case in human services (Fonagy and Higgitt, 1989).

Another important element in the selection of approach is consideration of specific techniques of data collection and generation that may be used. There are a number of standardised procedures and measures that can be employed. Coursey reports the use of a number of dimensions when selecting the measure:

> The measurements used should be: 1. Objective. 2. Repeatable by different observers at different times. 3. Efficient in terms of clear and mutually exclusive divisions, undistorted scale, and broad range of values to be recorded. 4. As simple, generally available, easily performed and inexpensive as possible. 5. Accurate in sensitivity and specificity. 6. Tested in pilot study. One could add to this list ... such considerations as validity, length of time to administer and score, the clients' and the staffs' sophistication in terms of vocabulary, familiarity with the scale's format and administration skill. (Coursey, 1977, p. 18)

A number of evaluation tools that meet these criteria are available, and 50 of those that assess the environmental aspects of human services have been well described in an annotated directory by Norma Raynes (1988). Examples of the types of measure that might be used include Program Analysis of Service Systems (PASS) (Wolfensberger and Glenn, 1975), a normalisation-based (q.v.) measure that consists of 50 areas that are assessed and rated by a team of trained and experienced raters, and which judges the degree to which the service being evaluated conforms to standards of service that would be expected in a service that followed normalisation principles. Areas assessed include administrative variables, such as the financial efficiency of the service, and the links it has with academic institutions; the type of image it portrays to the public about its clients; the effort put into integration of clients into the community, both socially and physically; the physical aspects of the environment in which the service is situated; and the effort put into developmental outcomes for clients. Other measures include socio-psychological measures such as the Ward Atmosphere Scale (Moos, 1974), and observational techniques such as the behavioural-based measures of engagement in appropriate activity used in evaluational research by, amongst others, Felce (1986), where the interaction between clients in a service and their carers and environment is observed.

Once again the selection of measures and methods depends on the defined purpose of the evaluation. Process-orientated measures, such as those of client engagement in activity, should be distinct from outcome-orientated measures, such as goal attainment scaling (Kiresuk and Sherman, 1968), and distinct again from more global measures of service performance such as PASS.

Stage Three: Carrying out the evaluation using the design and methods selected.

A number of problems can arise in carrying out the evaluation of a human service, however well designed and planned the evaluation procedure is. Twain (1975) lists some of the potential problem areas:

1. Ensuring that the funding and budgeting are managed and maintained.

2. Selecting and training evaluation staff, who may come from various disciplines.

3. Maintaining the quality of the evaluation process, including the reliability and consistency of data collection and recording.

4. Maintaining the separate integrity of the evaluation and of the program, so that the evaluation can remain as objective as possible, and as little contamination as possible of the program process occurs (except in models of evaluation where this may be desired).

5. Establishing and maintaining collaboration with program staff and clients.

6. Establishing routines for the collection and analysis of data.

Brunning, Cole and Huffington (1990) have presented a similar model for what they term "organisational development" consulting, which is similar to that of process consultancy, and mirrors, and can be applied to, the process of human service evaluation. They identify nine stages in this process:

1. *Scouting*: the evaluator decides whether or not to carry on with the evaluation.

2. *Entry*: the evaluator establishes a relationship with the service as a basis for completing the evaluation.

3. *Contracting*: a mutual contract, formal or informal, is developed, clarifying expectations and establishing a modus operandi.

4. *Data-gathering*: using the measures and techniques selected as pertinent to the service, data are gathered to enable evaluation to be completed.

5. *Diagnosis*: using the data to clarify the objectives set for the evaluation.

6. *Feedback*: relaying the findings of the evaluation back to the program or the sponsor of the evaluation.

7. *Intervention*: using the results to effect planned improvements in the service.

8. *Evaluation*: assessing the success of the evaluation process in bringing about desired or necessary change in the service.

9. *Withdrawal*: terminating the evaluation and withdrawing from the service, at the same time leaving the service with an enhanced capacity to introduce and manage change.

The same authors also present five caricatures of clinical psychologists as change agents that equally apply to evaluators, including the "gate crasher" (insensitive entry into the system), the "devil's advocate" (stultifying the process and the program by obsession with rigorous scientific methods), the "hero innovator" (failing to create a critical mass within the system and to gain credibility as an evaluator), the "agent provocateur" (fuelling internal conflict or taking sides) and the "fence sitter" (failure to offer concrete help as a result of the evaluation). The importance of handling the interpersonal aspects of the evaluation process sensitively is vital, as evaluation can be a threatening experience to those involved in the service, and the evaluator can be seen as an agent of management control.

Stage Four: Reporting the results.

The basic aim of any attempt at evaluation is to assess the performance of the service and then to modify it or suggest modifications that will increase the quality of the service. Consequently, the method, form and timing of presenting the feedback are crucial aspects of any evaluation. Coursey lists a number of reasons why evaluation results and recommendations are not implemented. These are:

1. The evaluation results do not match the informational needs of the decision makers or are not relevant to the level of decision that must be made.

2. The results are ambiguous or unclear.

3. The evaluator is reluctant to draw conclusions from his or her data.

4. The evaluation offers no recommendations about future possible improvements.

5. Dissemination of the report is poor. The report may be too large, too late, ineffectively presented or simply unreadable.

6. The evaluator may have no continuing commitment to the program once the evaluation is finished.

7. There may be many intraservice methods of avoiding implementation, including discrediting the findings, discounting the findings, blaming the victims (clients) or ignoring the results completely.

In order to increase the likelihood of implementation of evaluation results, Coursey summarises the research on this topic and lists a further nine points:

1. Evaluation results are best used when implementation implies only moderate alterations in processes, staffing or costs, or when few interests are threatened.

2. The early identification of potential users of the results and the selection of issues of concern to them should increase the use of data.

3. Evaluation should be integrated into the service's strategic planning and development process.

4. Both administrators and service staff should be involved throughout the evaluation process, to enable realistic expectations to be set, and joint ownership of the results.

5. Recommendations should centre on the process variables employed by the staff ("hows"), not on the staff themselves ("whos").

6. Results should be fed back whilst still relevant.

7. If the results are made known gradually in a phased program, and recommendations implemented in the same way, resistance to change may be less.

8. If evaluation is seen as an educative process, then the feedback should involve effective methods of presentation and dissemination.

9. Evaluators need to see their role not as external objective scientists, but as change consultants who are involved in the process of implementing the recommended changes to improve the service.

The process of evaluation is far more than just a research exercise, and requires involvement in the organisation in a way that, paradoxically, compromises the nature of evaluation as an objective science.

The Uses of Evaluation in Human Services

The detailed description of types of evaluation carried out in human services is beyond the scope of this book, as there are many examples and reviews in virtually every human service, including mental health (Coursey, Specter, Murrell and Hunt, 1977; Milne, 1987), education (Sanders, 1992), family services (Wells and Beagel, 1991) and learning disability services (Bradley and Bersani, 1990).

In the latter area, Dickens (1990) discusses service evaluation in the context of research approaches to quality assurance, and suggests that there are three main categories of evaluation research, which are typical of other fields as well. These categories are, firstly, observational research, which draws heavily on the in-vivo observation of the service in action, and is related to the body of work on staff interactions in human services. Landesman's work is a good example of this in the learning disabilities field (1987). This involves the detailed description of environments, naturalistic observation of the day-to-day behaviour and interactions of clients and an assessment of staff activities. In order to introduce a comparative element into the evaluations, she uses a randomisation design using matched controls. The findings indicate that quality of services to this client group may be person- and situation-specific, and not easily translatable into generalisable standards of care.

The second approach outlined by Dickens is the use of multivariate methods, which attempts to control for the massive number of variables affecting quality in service settings by using many measures and studying the interaction of these measures. Brown, Bayer and MacFarlane (1988) attempted to evaluate the effectiveness and quality of rehabilitation services, and the quality of life enjoyed by the clients, using this approach. They included measures such as psychometric tests, adaptive behaviour rating scales, quality of life questionnaires and evaluations of agency philosophy, goals and structure, including costs. Their results illustrate the importance of using both subjective and objective measures in assessing quality. A similar approach has been used by Mental Handicap in Wales— Applied Research Unit in their longitudinal evaluation of the Nimrod residential service for people with learning disability in Cardiff, Wales. (See the sequence of published reports by this Unit from 1985 to 1992.) They employed numerous measures, including psychometric tests, adaptive behaviour scales, observational measures of engagement, client questionnaires, scales assessing the physical environment and its maintenance, and also included a full PASS assessment (Williams, 1992). In the United States similar long-term evaluations have been carried out on people with learning disabilities leaving long-stay institutions, such as the one carried out in Vermont (Burchard, Hasazi and Gordon, 1989), and the studies of ex-residents of Pennhurst in Pennsylvania (Conroy and Bradley, 1985).

The last type of evaluation mentioned by Dickens concerns the use of one or more measurement tools, such as PASS. As we have already discussed above, PASS is an objective measure of the extent to which a service meets the criteria of normalisation. The results of using this type of measure have been reported elsewhere (Flynn, 1980), and generally are effective in achieving systemic change in services that either have already embraced the principles of normalisation, or are open to the concept. Other measures have also been used, and service evaluation packages are available for agencies to carry out their own evaluation (e.g. Bromsgrove and Redditch Health Authority, 1988). Similar measures exist in the field of mental health—for example the Model Standards Questionnaire for assessing mental health rehabilitation settings (Lavender, 1987), and for generic human service settings such as the ENQUIRE system (Richards and Heginbotham, 1992).

One interesting aspect of service evaluation is the increasing involvement of consumers in the evaluation process. The evaluation of Nimrod mentioned above using PASS had a client as one of the team members, an increasing trend in the use of the measure and its companion, PASSING. This is a reflection of the importance of consumer views on human services, which we will consider next. In conclusion it can be seen that evaluation and research techniques enable an external, scientific view of a service, but do not constitute the totality of a quality assurance system because, by definition, the evaluator is external to the processes and structures of the service. It is an important tool and technique of a total approach to quality, as we will see later.

CHAPTER 7

Tools and techniques of human service quality 3: Involving workers and consumers: quality circles and consumer views

INVOLVING PEOPLE: QUALITY CIRCLES IN HUMAN SERVICES

In a previous chapter we discussed the role of quality circles as a technique in the range of quality assurance and control tools. This approach differs from other tools and techniques of quality in that, as we have previously discussed, it stresses the interpersonal—the "soft" aspect of quality, as opposed to the "hard" aspects the previous two techniques above have implied. Given the bias of human services towards the prevalence of the interpersonal aspects of quality, it is not surprising that techniques such as quality circles should have found ready acceptance as a way of improving the quality of services provided.

Earlier we cited Oakland's (1989) definition of the essentials of quality circles, that is a group of workers who meet voluntarily, regularly, in normal working time, under the leadership of their "supervisor" to identify, analyse and solve work-related problems and to recommend solutions to management. One of the features of the use of quality circles in human services is the way in which this concept has been adapted to suit the situation of the service concerned, and the fact that many such adaptations involve the consumer in the process in a way that is unusual in manufacturing or other service industry applications. Barra (1989) gives an example of this and describes the use of quality circles in the Mercy Hospital of Pittsburgh, USA. Here the modifications were designed to accommodate the unique features of a health care setting, which he cites as an organisational structure that supports multiple independent hierarchies, the presence of a crisis-orientated environment, traditional dependence on a professional-discipline orientation rather than a product orientation, broad skill and educational level discrepancies amongst staff, an emphasis on professional interdependence and teamwork because of the nature of the function fulfilled, and a service environment that demands that the quality of care delivered to the patient be the focus of all quality initiatives. In order to function within these constraints, quality circles were developed that reflected these factors, and were composed of relevant staff from a multidisciplinary background. The types of quality issues tackled were:

1. A redesign of the system for sorting and allocating treatment to patients in the accident and emergency department.

2. Improved cooperation between hospital and city paramedics.

3. Substantial savings in the retrieval of lost supplies.

4. More productive station rotation plans for laboratory personnel.

5. An improved information system for more efficient management of patients' diets by dieticians.

Mercy Hospital staff were reported by Barra to have gained from the introduction of quality circles in terms of personal development, enhancement of the management–employee relationship, improved communication, increased job participation and job satisfaction.

In another field of human services, that of services for people with learning disability, there has been extensive work carried out on developing an approach to quality assurance and improvement based on the idea of quality circles. A booklet published by the Independent Development Council for People with Mental Handicaps (learning disability) in 1986, called *Pursuing Quality*, set out a framework for using the technique in services for this client group. The approach is based on a number of principles of service quality, and on a set of values similar to O'Brien's five service accomplishments. These quality principles are:

- Spend time with service users
- Focus on results rather than processes
- Concentrate on a few major areas where you can achieve substantial results
- Develop a common vision and common values
- Build on strengths and support what is good

Based on these principles, the authors suggest the formation of "Quality Action Groups", composed of the relevant stakeholders in the service in question. These people will include clients, families, service staff and managers, service planners, professional specialists, politicians and members of the local community. In forming each group it is important to specify the level at which it will operate, as this will determine the membership. A group focusing on a staffed house in the community might include the person in charge, some of the residents, neighbours and local residents, whilst a group focusing on the needs of the total client group would involve managers, planners from all relevant agencies, politicians and client representatives. The group, once established, then undertakes a number of tasks, including defining the service under review, defining what is meant by quality for the service, assessing what the service achieves for the clients, and then suggesting ways of improving the service or filling service gaps that become apparent. These suggestions for improvement should be expressed in the form of objective goals and outcomes, against which progress can be measured.

The booklet gives a number of examples of Quality Action Groups in action in various types of service in the field of learning disabilities. Howell, James and Abbott (1990) give a detailed description of the use of the approach in a small residential provision for young people with learning disabilities. Members of their group included residents, staff, parents, a psychologist and an educationalist. After agreeing a number of aims for the house and its residents (e.g. "The people who live at 11 Green Lane will make use of a wide range of community facilities"), the group meetings focused on actions required to meet these aims. The outcome benefits were seen to be:

1. Clear explicit statements of shared values.

2. Parents and staff were able to articulate and discuss differences openly, in a non-threatening atmosphere.

3. Service users made a number of personal accomplishments.

4. Staff morale and job satisfaction improved.

5. Parents felt more involved in the care process, and decisions concerning it.

It can be seen that there are a number of benefits in using this type of approach, including the facilitation of involvement of clients in their own services, the use of "external" people, including lay people, and an objective view of the service and the involvement of staff and stakeholders at all levels in determining the parameters of quality. On the other hand, the Quality Action Groups as described seem to exist in a vacuum, with little contact with other quality assurance schemes that might be being pursued locally or nationally, and they have an air of unrealism and artificiality about them, particularly where the use of lay people or neighbours is concerned. The booklet gives little guidance on the interpersonal aspects of Quality Action Group functioning, and no idea of methods of securing what may be fundamental service changes. The involvement of clients may also be difficult, if ways are not found to facilitate their active participation, and to ensure that their presence is not tokenism.

Øvretveit (1992), whilst not using the term "quality circle", discusses a similar methodology and gives an example based on a unidisciplinary staff group solving a problem concerning client records in a human service setting. He is against the use of untrained staff groups across many disciplines and using lay people in the process. He writes:

Untrained staff groups do not naturally take a systematic approach. They tend to fly into speculations about solutions without stating the problem properly, or define problems only in terms of assumed causes. This can lead to wasting time and money on the wrong things. (Øvretveit, 1992, p. 87)

He stresses the need to use the techniques involved in quality circles within the context of other techniques—particularly the one he calls the "quality correction cycle"—and a total quality management approach to changing human services.

CONSUMER VIEWS ON HUMAN SERVICES

Earlier in this book we devoted a large section to the role of the consumer in the judgement of the quality of service industries, and came to the conclusion that, in most services, quality can only adequately be defined from the viewpoint of the consumer. In this section of our present discussion of the tools and techniques of quality assurance in human services, we will look at this role and how it has been implemented in some of the human service areas that have already featured throughout our discussion, namely those of health and social care in their widest aspects.

There are a number of difficulties around this discussion that arise from some of the features of human services that we also examined earlier in this book. Often it is difficult to decide who is the consumer of any particular service. Many human services, particularly those for children, old people or the mentally disordered, work on a system of "proxy consumer", whereby someone acting on behalf of the person chooses, purchases, arranges, and coordinates the health or social care being offered as a service. This person might be an agent of the service itself—a care manager arranging a day care place perhaps, or a general practitioner arranging a hospital admission—or they might be a relative or friend. Sometimes, in advanced service systems, there may be a number of interested lay people who act on behalf of persons where they are deemed to be incapable of acting for themselves. These people are termed "citizen advocates", or they may be legal guardians. Another difficulty in human services is the related fact that choice of service is often limited, or is dominated by a monopoly supplier so that there is no choice whatsoever. The type of consumerism that is possible in many manufacturing and retail settings, where the customers have the ultimate say in the quality of the product by virtue of their purchasing decision, does not apply. There is only one service available in many settings for any particular client group so the appropriate cliché is "take it or leave it".

The consumerist movement in human services began in Western countries some time in the 1960s, and found expression in organisations such as "Greenpeace" and the Consumers' Association, and in the writings of Ralph Nader in the United States, who exposed the lack of safety concern in US motor manufacturers and influenced legislation to remedy this. At the same time, in human service, a view was growing that human services, and the professionals in human services, far from being benign and useful influences on people's welfare, were causing problems rather than solving them. Haug and Sussman (1969), for example, suggested that clients began to distrust professionals because of the professionals' attempted control over aspects of the patients' lives and care that lay beyond the professionals' proper concern, and they became dissatisfied with the care given because of incompetence or mistaken efforts within the professionals' proper range of concern. Illich (1987), and particularly the chapter in the same book by John McGhee, develop this view into one that blames professionals for "iatrogenic illness" (illness caused by the treatment), and "disabling professions", whose primary effect is to remove self-esteem and competence in their consumers. McGhee writes:

> As service professions gain the power to unilaterally define remedy, need and code the service process ... [the] servicers define the output of their service in accordance with their own satisfaction with the result. Increasingly, professionals are claiming the power to decide whether their "help" is effective. The important, valued and evaluated outcome of service is the professional's assessment of his own efficacy. The client is viewed as a deficient person, unable to know whether he has been helped. This ... premise is contested by the consumer movement ... Professionally managed service systems are now dealing with this remnant citizen role as consumer. The result has been an increasing professional focus on manipulating consumer perceptions of outcomes. (McGhee, 1987, pp. 87–88)

Hollander (1980) wrote of a fundamental change in mental health services brought about by a "mental health revolution" challenging "uncritical acceptance of expert direction".

Some of the outcomes of these factors are our concern here. One avenue pursued was that of pressure group formation and legislation—particularly in the United States—which has had a considerable effect on the shape and form of some human services, mainly those with institutional residential care at their heart. (For example see Lottman, 1990.) Another avenue, which is more germane to the present topic, was an increasing move to monitor and evaluate human service quality by seeking out and acting upon the views of human service consumers—mainly those who are directly involved in the transaction at its "frontline"—the clients, patients, residents and recipients of health and social care. Such moves now have government blessing, and are an essential feature of most human service quality procedures, at least in health care, and increasingly in social care. A related issue is that of "user participation", which is something more than consumer evaluation, but includes consumers acting in a planning capacity, and even in management roles in human services. (See for example Smith, 1988.) There is a continuum of such involvements, running from total participation—that is the users run the service (for example a self-help group for sufferers of agoraphobia)—to total non-participation (for example a high-tech medical setting). Quite often these two aspects—consumer participation and consume evaluation—become confused. In the present discussion, which is to do with the tools and techniques of quality assurance, we will look at some attempts made to measure the views of consumers, with special reference to health care, and not at ways in which consumers can participate in the planning and running of human services, although it is realised that this separation may well be an artificial one. This is well illustrated in the book by Williamson (1992), from which we have already quoted. This takes a very broad view of consumerism, and switches between the means of expression of consumer views and the participation of users in service by way of consumer specification of service standards in health care. We will examine purely the mechanisms used in a number of studies for examining consumer views of health care, mental health care and services for people with learning disability, and will not be too concerned with the findings and the meaning of them.

The basic tools and techniques of measuring customer views fall into five categories:

1. *Measuring customer dissatisfaction*: this concentrates on facilitating customer complaints, and installing a process for the analysis of complaints and learning from them. This is a popular approach in many human services, which may have statutory complaints procedures. Its main drawback is that it focuses on the negative aspects of quality, and tends to lead to the allocation of blame, rather than the remedying of problems.

2. *Surveys of customers' views*: these may be large-scale, that is carried out on large national samples (for example the recent NOP survey of patients' views of the NHS in Scotland) or may be local efforts, sometimes using standardised measures, but often using unstructured or poorly designed questionnaires. The advantages lie in the quantification possible, and the disadvantages lie in the usual areas for survey work: base rates, sample error, poor response rates and questionnaire bias.

3. *Focus groups*: these small groups of customers, and often non-customers, are set up to discuss the nature of the service and how it can be improved. They are similar to the Quality Action Groups we have mentioned already. Their advantage is the amount of information gleaned, and the opportunity to develop a discussion on a topic. The disadvantages are the effects of the group process on the course and content of the discussion.

4. *Critical incident analysis*: this technique is a development of the complaints approach, and asks people to focus on good and bad experiences of services, to define features that may be important in developing quality. This approach can also be integrated into routine clinical audit, using the "occurrence screening" approach common in the United States (Stevens and Bennett, 1989). Advantages include the possibility of focusing on positive as well as negative aspects of quality, but disadvantages lie in an over-reliance on "incident"—that is non-conforming aspects of service provision.

5. *Flow-process analysis*: Øvretveit (1992) describes this technique which follows the customer through a service delivery process, and identifies actual and potential problems at each stage, based on the balance between customer perception, expectations and experience. Its advantages include the clarification of the service process into discrete stages and the consideration of

the process from the point of view of the consumer. Its disadvantages include the over-simplification of the complex nature of most human services.

Consumer Views on Health Care

Systematic attempts to obtain the views of health care consumers—patients—date from the late 1950s, with the publication of a seminal work in the United States, by Abdellah and Levine (1957). They were interested in patients' assessment of nursing practice, and developed a system for asking specific questions about 50 possible causes of dissatisfaction, and weighting the answers to provide a crude measure of the efficiency of nursing care. Unfortunately it actually measures nursing inefficiency, and is biased towards a negative view of quality—dissatisfaction rather than satisfaction. Since this early work there have been a number of attempts to produce a workable system of sampling patients' views on health care. Problems in this endeavour include the lack of available, standardised, reliable and valid tools; the difficulty of dealing with the resulting data and translating the findings into action; and the problems of convincing professionals—particularly doctors—that the views of the patients on the health care they receive have any validity whatsoever.

A British attempt to devise a standardised measure of patients' views comes from the work in Manchester of Brian Moores and Andy Thompson (Moores and Thompson, 1986; Thompson, 1986). Their work falls into a number of phases. Firstly, they sampled the views of a number of patients to ascertain the issues of concern, rather than accepting the professionals' perception of these views. To do this they conducted in-depth unstructured interviews with discharged patients, using a cold-calling technique, and asking people to talk generally about their stay in hospital. Secondly, they again used a cold-calling technique with discharged patients, but this time they used a pilot structured questionnaire based on the first phase, in order to refine the content. The third phase involved translating the interview schedules and responses into a written form of fixed choice questionnaire, acknowledging the drawbacks of such techniques such as low response rates, lack of scope for open-ended questions and problems with reading and language levels. This questionnaire was then tested on a random sample of discharged patients, and refined in terms of psychometric and statistical properties, until a final version was produced, which consisted of a 32-page A5 booklet, *What The Patient Thinks*. This measures six factors of patient satisfaction, derived from a factor analysis of the total questionnaire. These are:

- Medical care and information

- Physical aspects and food

- Non-tangible environment ("atmosphere")

- Nursing care

- Quantity of food

- Visiting arrangements

The questionnaire has been used in a number of hospital settings, and its factor structure and standardisation provide reliable data on the views of patients. It also allows interhospital comparisons to be made, in much the same way as PIs. The major problems are its length and complexity—it takes a long time to complete and the results are complex and present difficulties in translating into management action.

These problems have led to the search for a shorter, more reliable questionnaire tool which will give information on patient views. One such example is that produced by the CASPE project (Clinical Accountability, Service Planning and Evaluation), called PATSAT. This is a computer-based system, which measures 12 very basic areas of concern, including satisfaction with treatment by doctors and nurses, the quality of the ward environment and food and the information given whilst in hospital. It is given to patients whilst they are still in hospital, and asks them to rate the dimensions on a four-point scale of satisfaction ranging from very satisfied to very dissatisfied. Its main positive aspects include the ease of data collection, the ease of scoring, and the availability of information for management in the form of histograms with which to compare relative performance across and within hospitals. PATSAT has been heavily criticised, notably by Carr-Hill, Dixon and Thompson (1989) who regard it as far too simple, statistically invalid and insensitive, and structurally restrictive. They state that:

The components of satisfaction monitored by the CASPE index are a restricted set, perhaps insensitive to the substantial variations in satisfaction, and certainly likely to be insensitive to variations over time. Overall it is perhaps too simple and formal a tool to provide detailed and valid information. From the patient's point of view, a routine method is likely to provide only the most formal sorts of feedback—based on the provider's agenda. (Carr-Hill, Dixon and Thompson, 1989, p. 729)

The same criticisms would seem to apply to most attempts at measuring patient satisfaction in health settings, including the uses of the SERVQUAL tool that we referred to in an earlier chapter, and which has been adapted to a health setting. Thompson (1986) and Hurst and Ball (1990) have reviewed patient satisfaction studies, and reached similar conclusions. In addition they mention factors such as the "intimidation factor", which leads to patients being afraid to give negative answers during the course of their care in case of reprisals; positive response bias, where only satisfied patients respond; and the cost of data collection.

Consumer Views on Mental Health Services

In parallel with this development of the measurement of consumer views on general health treatment, there has been increasing emphasis on obtaining the views of users of mental health services. It is in this field that we encounter the cross-relationship between consumer views on quality of service and the concept of user participation, and most reviews on the topic, such as those by Anderson (1991) and McIver (1991), alternate between the two. To some extent this is motivated by the suggestion that increasing collaboration will enable better evaluation of services, because of the incorporation of consumer issues. Anderson distinguishes between "provider-led, user-oriented" evaluation, where the process is engendered by the provider of services but is focused on user's views, and "user-led, user-oriented" evaluation, where the client is the basic instigator of both parts, as a way of incorporating the two ideas.

Once again there are significant difficulties in obtaining consumer views in the field of mental health. There is a major effect of acquiescence, where questions will be answered according to the way in which they are asked, and there are problems in obtaining information from people whose cognitive processes may be extremely disturbed, and their hold on reality tenuous. Conventional methods of obtaining consumer views such as surveys and complaints procedures are not robust enough to cope with these potential difficulties. Despite this there is growing evidence of the successful collection of the views of people with mental health problems on their treatment in a variety of settings. One of the earliest attempts to do this was the work in London of Raphael (1974), who tried out three methods of data collection on hospital in-patients, including an individual interview, a complex questionnaire and a simple questionnaire. The latter was found to produce the best results, and Raphael reported that this was despite the presence of active psychiatric symptoms. Weinstein (1979), reviewing the results of a number of American studies, concluded that it was possible to use questionnaire measures to obtain the views of mental health service users, and that such views were often overwhelmingly positive. Anderson (1991) mentions the "halo effect" as a feature of this, where there is a reluctance to criticise carers, and a preference for "grateful testimonials" or idealised statements about mental health care experiences. In his review, Anderson also quoted a number of potential confounding factors that require consumer evaluations to be treated with care. These include the unidimensionality of satisfaction measured, with no possibility of discriminating between the user, treatment and therapist variables that would provide valid data; highly selected subject groups; low response rates; positively biased instruments; and characteristics of the interview favouring positive responses. Some ways around these factors are suggested in McIver's practical monograph (1991).

One of the most extensive reviews of the results and methodologies of assessing the views of consumers in mental health services was carried out by LeBow (1982). He lists a number of potential drawbacks found in the published studies to that date:

1. Lack of information on reliability.

2. Problems of validity: sampling errors, low response rates, lack of control over procedure, distortion in responses, lack of precise meaning of terminology used, inclusion of non-satisfaction items.

3. Utilitarian problems: lack of variability in responses, lack of variability across aspects of treatment, absence of accepted or comparable measures, failure to identify baselines for satisfaction, failure to differentiate between clients and between treatments, method variance, primitive data analysis and reporting.

Despite these problems LeBow is able to summarise the research and show positive evidence concerning the levels and type of satisfaction with treatment in many settings. He also discusses four criticisms of consumer research:

1. There are significant validity problems.

2. The results are not functionally useful, because of the tendency to bias and lack of variability in responses.

3. Consumers cannot adequately judge treatment, because they are inherently involved in the treatment process and their views may be coloured by aspects of their presenting condition.

4. Effectiveness data are the only reasonable evidence of quality or treatment outcome, and satisfaction is an irrelevant variable.

LeBow thinks that all these arguments have some merit, but that there are many counter-arguments that can be offered as alternative views, and which emphasise the importance of the consumer's viewpoint. His arguments include the fact that methodological imperfections can be overcome, using other methods and valid, reliable instruments; there is sufficient evidence that programme participants have a vital view of their treatment, despite their involvement in the process and their mental state; and satisfaction is an important mediating variable, alongside treatment effectiveness. In summary he writes:

> Consumer evaluation is found to be a useful though flawed method of assessing services, and it should be included in a multimethod treatment evaluation. (LeBow, 1982, p. 244)

Consumer Views on Learning Disability Services

The difficulties mentioned above in obtaining the views of users of mental health services apply equally in obtaining the views of people with learning disabilities about the services they use. Once again, there is a body of evidence to show that such views are obtainable, using adequate methodology, and that these views are a valid and vital part of quality assurance.

Two strands in approaching this are evident. One is the development of methods of obtaining information from users who have learning disability, and whose cognitive skills and levels of expressive and receptive communication may be low, and their literacy non-existent. The work of Margaret Flynn is important, and a good example of this (Flynn, 1986; Flynn and Saleem, 1986). Drawing on the published research on obtaining information from people with learning disabilities, she was able to conduct a content analysis of the replies to gain dimensions of satisfaction with local authority day care services, and of people's quality of life. She suggests some guidelines based on considerable American research to enable the adequate sampling of views:

1. The communication level of the participants should be established, and alternative question formats included.

2. Interviews should be taped to avoid the discomfort and anxiety induced by writing during the interview.

3. The question format and order should be flexible and responsive.

4. Open-ended questions should be avoided, and multiple choice questions may be better, with probes for additional information.

5. Use of pictures aids responsiveness.

6. Validity must be checked by questioning carers and significant others.

7. The presence of their families and/or carers significantly alters the answers people give.

8. Abstract questions, such as time- and frequency-based items, should be avoided.

Similar guidance has been incorporated into a number of evaluation studies where consumer views have been collected, such as that by Conroy, Walsh and Feinstein (1987).

A second strand, which we mentioned earlier in this chapter, is the participation of clients with learning disabilities in the evaluation of service systems instigated by external evaluators, or by services themselves. The inclusion of a client in the PASS evaluation of the NIMROD residential service was reported. A more extensive example is the evaluation of social-work-run day and residential services in London by the People First group of people with learning disabilities, reported by Whittaker, Gardner and Kershaw (1991). These evaluations were strongly based on a normalisation approach, and used the "Five Service Accomplishments" of O'Brien (1986) as their basis. Resulting from this was a multimodal evaluation using observation, interviews and structured questionnaires, taking pictures and playing informative games. Administration and responses to these were facilitated by using pictorial formats. The conclusions reached included some guidance for conducting user-led evaluations:

1. There is a need for commitment from service managers to support the evaluation and take its findings seriously.

2. Commitment is needed from "grass-roots" staff in facilitating the evaluation and valuing it and its participants.

3. Service users must be involved right from the start.

4. The right support must be provided, in terms of personal and advisory support for individuals involved, and practical and logistical assistance.

5. Plenty of preparation time must be allowed to prepare materials, develop participants' skills and allow them to get to know the services and the people in them.

6. The consultants who have learning difficulties in skills such as public speaking and assertiveness must be trained.

7. Teamwork must be stressed.

8. The ownership of the evaluation by the service users must be retained.

Conclusion

This section has stressed the importance of measuring the views of consumers of human services, and also expressed a number of potential and actual problems in pursuing such an approach.

These difficulties are no more, however, than those experienced when assessing the views of any consumer group. The overwhelming evidence is not only that such views are the sole basis for the assessment of the quality of services, but that tools and techniques exist that can overcome many of the difficulties identified.

In the last three chapters we have reviewed many of the techniques and tools of quality assurance that are conventionally found in human services, especially in health care. The use of these techniques is often in isolation from others, with one technique seen as the sole requirement for a quality measurement and assurance system. In the next chapter we will look at comprehensive systems of quality assurance in human services, that to a greater or lesser extent attempt to combine some of the methods we have discussed in these chapters into a coherent whole.

CHAPTER 8   Quality systems in human services

The techniques and tools mentioned above constitute component parts of any comprehensive system of quality assurance for human services, but do not provide, as individual techniques, an adequate basis on which to judge or improve quality. Despite this, various claims have been made to that end, and systems of quality assurance have been suggested that involve only one tool or technique. One way of viewing this was suggested by Dalley (1989). Writing about quality in the health care service sector, she reported on an analysis of various quality schemes in the NHS at that time, and distinguished three types of initiative: *quality assurance*, a management system for ensuring quality of care; *quality enhancement/ improvement*, a programme for evaluating quality and improving standards within available resources; *quality initiatives*, individual projects aimed at assessing and improving specific aspects of quality of care. Many of the initiatives fall into the last category, with few being placed either in the context of an overall quality assurance system or within a framework of total quality management. A number of authors have, however, summarised the essential qualities of a comprehensive system of quality assurance in various areas of human services. We will review some of them below, as examples, and then consider the impact, or potential impact, of BS5750/ISO9000 on human services. Finally, we will look at the topic of total quality management in human services, and suggest an extension of a model that we examined earlier in the book to the human service field, and in particular the therapeutic professions.

QUALITY ASSURANCE

Quality Assurance in Mental Health

In the field of mental health services, Clifford, Leiper, Lavender and Pilling (1989) after reviewing the literature in their field, set out what they see as the principles of a comprehensive system, which they then use to construct such a system, called QUARTZ. These principles are:

1. *Monitoring and enhancement should be compatible.* The elements that are chosen for monitoring should be those that will best lead to effective intervention, or are crucial to the development of quality in the service. Decisions on items to be monitored should be collaborative ones between management and staff, and staff should thereby be encouraged to own the system and implement its results.

2. *Elements of both internal and external review are necessary.* Internal review encourages staff to be involved, whilst external review promotes the value of objectivity and the relationship of the service to others that are similar.

3. *The value of facilitation must be acknowledged.* A non-managerial outsider who can guide and integrate the quality assurance process is essential, and the selection of the facilitator is an important aspect of the system.

4. *Quality assurance procedures should include an element of objectivity.* This might include a number of methods such as written guidelines for service evaluation, objective data collection and the use of formal analytical techniques.

5. *Quality assurance is only effective in the context of stated goals and priorities.* Values, philosophies and methods arising from them need to be considered as part of the system.

6. *Management commitment should be reflected in management practice.* Not only should managers be closely involved in the process of quality assurance, but they should also integrate the findings with strategic goals, and also give a commitment to act on the results.

7. *Quality is multifaceted.* Quality assurance processes should therefore reflect a wide range of definitions and aspects of

quality, with a degree of comprehensiveness and consideration of alternative views of quality. This will discourage an emphasis on one aspect of quality or of quality assurance techniques, to the detriment of others.

8. *Information should promote action.* The information gained through the system should form the agenda for action, and should be structured and analysed so as to influence and suggest courses of remedial action.

9. *A comprehensive approach is both possible and desirable.* A quality assurance system should be generalisable across a number of different settings and contexts, if it concentrates on basic process variables. Similarly the system should look not only at component parts of the system but at the system as a whole in the context within which it operates.

10. *Outcome must be assessed.* In human service quality assurance, the effect of the service on its target group is a vital aspect of the quality of that service.

11. *The system should aim to create dialogue between service users and providers.* Users should be seen as integral parts of the quality assurance system, and hence of the service itself.

12. *The system should anticipate difficulty in creating and managing change.* This includes the provision of adequate resources for the system to operate effectively, and commitment on the part of staff to making it work. The system itself should therefore be relatively easy to operate, balancing time and resource constraints with comprehensiveness and effectiveness.

The QUARTZ system develops these essential characteristics, and consists of five stages. These are:

1. A clear commitment on the part of management to the principles and values of the service, and the determination of a quality strategy to implement them.

2. The selection and training of a quality review team composed of professionals from all parts of the service, who act as review consultants.

3. The quality review of a service setting using a set of structured schedules identifying aspects of quality that are relevant to the

mental health field. These schedules are the central component of QUARTZ, and cover four main areas:

Resources and environments, including the physical setting and staff resources and finance.

External links, with the community, other agencies and administrative and professional management.

Management practices, including team functioning, client rules and policies and procedures of care.

Client review, including data on service usage, the views of clients, review of individual case outcomes and the content of service agreements.

4.   The review team and the staff in the service, in collaboration, use the information and conclusions derived from the schedules to produce a report on the service, which includes objectives and an action plan to remedy deficiencies.

5.   This stage involves the monitoring of progress by the review team in conjunction with staff in relation to the goals set in the previous step and the identification and review of new issues that might arise as the process continues.

The last three steps form the cycle of quality assurance and annual review. Data for the completion of the schedules come from a variety of sources and use a variety of methods, including observation, staff interview, questionnaires, review of records, and client interviews.

QUARTZ is an interesting system of quality assurance in that it attempts to combine both "hard" and "soft" features of quality management into an integrated whole, with its consideration of both the interpersonal processes ("soft" variables) and the use of objective techniques of data collection ("hard" variables). It also considers the importance of an organisation-wide approach to quality, as does total quality management.

Quality Assurance in Health Services

One of the most comprehensive systems for quality assurance within a health services context has been described by Christopher Wilson in *Hospital-wide Quality Assurance* (1987). His approach is based on the definition of quality assurance from the Canadian Council on Hospital Accreditation that we mentioned in the last chapter, and on an organisational structure that stresses the importance of, and includes, the hospital board of management, the managers themselves, a steering committee of the adoption of the quality assurance process, the medical staff and lastly all other departments and services. The introduction of his system consists of six stages, which he terms an "adult learning model", and comprises:

1. Documenting existing quality management procedures.

2. Improving the recognition of quality in the performance of the hospital and its staff.

3. Incorporating into the structure, organisation and policies of the hospital strategies for assuring quality.

4. Assessing performance against explicit standards.

5. Planning criteria-based audits of all principal functions of the hospital.

6. Using the quality assurance committee to endorse quality improvement plans.

These steps also interact with various cycles of quality assurance activity, based on the type of quality assurance cycle we have seen before.

Wilson thinks that there are four essential components of quality assurance in his system, some of which comprise a number of elements. These are:

1. *Setting objectives*

   This component is divided into two elements, *performance standards* and *management goals*. The foundation of all quality assurance systems must begin with the establishment of goals, which are defined as "a future objective, which may be general and not well defined". They set the overall thrust of the system and of the hospital, and are used for general direction by management. On the other hand performance standards are definitions of attainment that can be met, and cover important elements of performance. Performance standards can come from a number of sources: *external*, including mandatory standards such as legislation and standards set by regulatory agencies and academic bodies, and prescriptive standards such as manufacturer's advice and voluntary codes of practice; and *internal*, including the goals mentioned above, administrative procedures and policies and job descriptions and procedures.

2. *Quality promotion*

    This section of Wilson's system concentrates on the issue of improving personal standards of performance of staff and includes staff training and development; continuing professional development; staff appraisal; suggestion procedures; quality assessment procedures; and two non-staff-related activities, product evaluation and preventive maintenance procedures. This section of the system will not be subject to the same rigorous measurement as other parts of it.

3. *Activity monitoring*

    Two methods monitor the performance of the hospital in quality terms. The first of these is *quality control*, which consists of a list of activities that are carried out routinely by various parts of the hospital system, such as annual checking of credentials, regular fire drills, performance appraisal programmes, regular testing of equipment, etc. Wilson also considers occurrence screening (q.v.) and nursing audit (q.v.) within this section. The other aspect to activity monitoring is that of *quality supervision*, which covers two aspects of management activity and performance: inspection and incident handling.

4. *Performance assessment*

    The fourth part of Wilson's system covers the measurement and evaluation of performance. This is done in three ways. *Quality review* means a process of monitoring and analysis of regularly collected data to yield indications of the quality of care or service, and to suggest areas for improvement. This activity may be carried out with reference to the predetermined standards, and may be less structured or informal. *Quality evaluation* is another term for audit, and is a form of self-appraisal of performance on defined criteria against predetermined standards, and is based on the formal evaluation of objective data. Quality approval is the stage of the quality assurance process that incorporates the views of others external to the system, and contrasts with the former two categories that stress self-assessment. In this element, the views of external accreditation agencies and bodies, academic bodies and most importantly the clients of the service are sought.

Wilson sees these four essential components as being in a linear and sequential relationship. Quality assurance begins with goals and standards (1), which must be promulgated and the necessary skills developed (2), their attainment has to be monitored (3), and finally the entire product has to be evaluated (4). At the same time the four elements interact, so a simple linear relationship may not be adequate to describe the functioning of this system.

In describing the system of quality assurance set out above, Wilson has made a major contribution to the pragmatics of setting up and maintaining a comprehensive way of improving quality, and his book is recommended as a useful text and source of ideas for implementing quality assurance in health and other human service systems. What is apparent, however, is the emphasis it places on mechanisms, or techniques, to the detriment of people, which parallels the criticisms of similar systems in other service industries, and points to the need for the consideration of the interactional processes of quality improvement that form a major part of total quality management. It also does not stress values and rights, and the paramount contribution that the consumer makes to the judgement of quality.

Quality Assurance Systems in Learning Disability Services

One area of human service that is of particular interest is that of service to people with learning difficulties (previously "mental handicap" or "mental retardation"). This is because services to these people are often provided by a number of agencies, representative of different types of human service concerns. There might be general lessons to be learnt from this service area as a result.

The subject of quality assurance in services for the client group variously labelled "people with a mental handicap" or "developmentally disabled" or "people with learning disabilities" has been reviewed in a number of places, including Dickens (1990, 1991) and in a collection of papers edited by Bradley and Bersani (1990) that is recognised as the major text on the subject.

As we have already seen above, Dickens distinguishes three approaches to quality assurance in services for this client group, based on *administrative* reasons, *research* considerations and *humanitarian* concern. He also reviews various ways of approaching quality, and defines three areas that need to be considered in any comprehensive quality assurance system:

1. *Quality of service*, which includes the environmental aspects of the service, its management style and organisation structure, the philosophical and value base of the service and the resources it uses for the clients it services. It can be measured and quantified by structured questionnaires and observation.

2. *Quality of care*, which is concerned with the interactional process between staff and clients, the systems and methods employed to provide the service and staff competence. It is measured by observational techniques, particularly participant observation.

3. *Quality of life*, which represents the goal of the service and the desired outcome of its efforts on behalf of clients. It is measured by satisfaction measures and outcomes.

Bradley (1990) considers that there are a number of realistic objectives for any adequate quality assurance system for human services, particularly those that deal with people with learning disabilities. These are:

1. To assure that providers of human services have the capability to provide an acceptable level of service.

2. To assure that client services are provided consistent with accepted beliefs about what constitutes good practice.

3. To assure that a commitment of resources provides a reasonable level of service from the point of view of the consumer as well as of the one supplying the funds.

4. To assure that the services provided have the intended effect.

5. To assure that the limited supply of services is provided to clients most in need.

6. To assure that the legal and human rights of people with disabilities are protected.

Bradley then outlines four areas that must be targeted by quality assurance systems:

1. *Inputs*: these are the structural measures of the service, including the physical facility, the nature of the clients being served, the number and competency of the staff and the regulatory framework within which the service is delivered. Inputs are relatively easy to measure, and represent the earliest attempts at a quality control process.

2. *Process*: this area concerns the interaction between client and organisation, and may be assessed by observation or consideration of documentation.

3. *Outputs*: this is synonymous with "product" and includes such things as the number of clients served or discharged. It is also relatively easy to measure.

4. *Outcomes*: this is the end product or culmination of service delivery and is a measure of the effect or impact that the service delivered has on its clients. The measurement of outcomes is difficult, and often ignored by quality assurance systems, mainly because of the difficulties of attributing causality.

Kimmich (1990) reports on a system of quality assurance based on the above schema that was developed in South Carolina for the State Health and Human Services Finance Commission which has responsibility for the state's social services, youth services, drug and alcohol abuse services and mental retardation (learning disability) services. The implementation of the schema involved five essential steps:

Step 1: Understanding the system, which involved mapping the existing quality assurance techniques used, determining which aspects of quality assurance were already well dealt with, determining how the service process actually occurred and producing a thorough analysis of the data collected from this step.

Step 2: This step involved developing standards, which form the basis for the rest of the system, and have been established on a collaborative basis, with all involved in service provision. This sequence of activities started with defining the service, developing a philosophy for the service and including the who, what, why, when, where and how of service provision. Secondly, the standards were written using a matrix that ensured all aspects of the service enterprise were covered. This matrix is formed by two dimensions. The first of these are the types of standards that correlate with five fundamental goals of quality assurance. Specifically they are:

- *Input*—to assure capability

- *Process*—to assure good practice

- *Output*—to assure productivity

- *Outcome*—to assure effectiveness

- *Need*—to assure service to those most in need

The second element covers six aspects of service provision and good programme management, which are: human resources, facility, client, services, administrative and fiscal concerns, and community relations. Both elements, forming a matrix, were used to formulate standards—written statements defining a quality service—and indicators, which were a measurable definition of that standard.

Step 3: In this step measurement approaches were developed. These included self-measurement inventories, on-site monitoring visits and information from central-state-level sources.

Step 4: Here controls and enhancements were developed, stressing feedback from the previous step to the services so that service delivery could be improved. This is done in an enhancing, not a critical way.

Step 5: The most important aspect of the system is this step which concentrated on developing a communication structure within which quality assurance issues could be tackled and information passed on to services for them to further enhance their work.

In her conclusions regarding the implementation of this system, Kimmich outlines three essential lessons that have been learnt. Firstly, the philosophy of quality assurance must be explained again and again, with opportunities provided for individuals and services to renew their definition and vision of quality. Secondly, political leadership is necessary, and this is needed over a sustained period. Thirdly, local service providers must be continually involved in both development and implementation stages. The work of Bradley and the description of its implementation by Kimmich show a comprehensive framework within which quality can be assured and developed, and one which is based heavily on a standards-type approach.

BS5750/ISO9000 AND HUMAN SERVICES

In the previous chapter the content of BS5750/ISO9000 for service industries was outlined and some issues concerning it were discussed. In this section we will not examine the standard in detail, but will consider some of the implications it has for human services. As yet BS5750/ISO9000 has made only a minimal impact in the human services field, but there is an increasing trend towards discussion of its ramifications and more evidence of human service systems gaining recognition under it. Amongst the human services that have achieved this are a health centre and general medical practice, a nursing home, some further education centres, hospitals, and an ambulance service. Dickens and Horne (1991), writing at the start of the introduction of the British Standard into health services, suggested that:

> BS5750/ISO9000 has had a major impact on industry, and its achievement is seen as an award which carries high status. It will be interesting to see if it has the same effect on the NHS. Perhaps in the future we will see purchasers specifying BS5750/ISO9000 as the standard contractual condition on QA systems for provider agencies. (Dickens and Horne, 1991, p. 25)

Ellis (1988), discussing the earlier version of BS5750/ISO9000, that for manufacturing industry, draws attention to four items that seem to have importance within that version for health care organisations. These are:

1. The requirement for an objectively documented quality assurance system.

2. The need for regular review—perhaps external—of the system.

3. The need for corrective action on deficiencies highlighted by the review.

4. The need to train staff not only about quality but also in the system's operation.

Rooney (1988), again writing in terms of the basic manufacturing industry version of the standard, took a pragmatic view, and attempted to determine whether basic elements of BS5750/ISO9000 were already present, or could be adapted to suit, four health care service settings in the English Midlands. The features she examined were: information transfer, traceability, feedback loops, documented records, standards, identification of non-conforming service, and corrective action. From the survey she carried out, she concluded that many of the above features were present in one form or another, or could be developed by extending existing features. Most of them did not form a part of a coherent system of quality assurance, such as suggested by BS5750/ISO9000, and she suggested that certain types of health care service were more suited to this than others. These included purchasing, pharmacy, catering, laboratories and medical engineering.

Building on this work, Robertson (1992) has extended Rooney's analysis of BS5750/ISO9000 to suit nursing applications. She sees this as a logical extension of the work already described on standards and monitoring and nursing, and an important part of the implementation of total quality management in a nursing context. She sets out the full text of BS5750/ISO9000 in a version for nursing practice, and also draws attention not only to the content issues, but also to the process ones, with suggestions for the introduction of a quality system, and some of the timescales involved. (Robertson estimates two to three years for a general hospital.)

Øvretveit (1990, 1992) has criticised the use or impending use of BS5750/ISO9000 in health service settings. He cites a number of reasons for this. Firstly, he thinks that the system is too complicated for health settings, where most services are just beginning to come to terms with the basics of quality assurance. Secondly, he is not convinced about the benefits of accreditation when weighed against the costs, particularly in the light of the first point, that is, the early stage at which most health services currently function. Thirdly, he suggests that the introduction of the standard could risk discrediting a quality approach with staff who are not used to the type of discipline the system imposes, particularly the emphasis on documentation, where considerable need for documentation (e.g. patient records) already exists. His overall conclusion is that simpler systems should be used first, before BS5750/ISO9000, and he suggests the use of the Malcolm Baldridge criteria from the United States.

In other areas of human services, however, considerable efforts are going into the translation of the BS5750/ISO9000 criteria into workable quality assurance systems, and into gaining accreditation under the scheme. St John-Brooks (1993) reported on the modification of the wording to suit a further education college over an 18-month period. Examples of the translation required included the substitution of "curriculum design, development and delivery" for "process control", and "diagnostic for client/course failure" for "control of non-conforming product". Once again the date of the college in question's registration, May 1991, suggests that more adaptation than is presently necessary was required, because of the use of the earlier version of the standard.

As we have previously said, the full effect of BS5750/ISO9000 on human services has yet to be seen. It offers a number of attractions both to purchasers and to providers, including the opportunity to demand a detailed specification for a quality assurance system in contracts, providing a solid framework on which to build a quality approach, the advantage of external assessment, and improved performance through its implementation. On the other hand doubts have been raised regarding the suitability of the standard in its present form, the amount of documentation required in already document-intensive services, the problem of choosing an assessor with the requisite experience, and the question of whether such a system is too complex for the present state of most human services' quality assurance efforts.

Lastly, the question must be asked of human services—why bother? As we have seen, the research tends to point to market and competitive advantage as one of the main perceived benefits of having BS5750/ISO9000 certification. In human services, although they are now subject to market forces, the monopoly held by most service providers means that such accreditation is unnecessary. People are hardly likely to say about a nursing home: "Granny will be happier there—they've got BS5750/ISO9000". The restricted choice that applies for most consumers and agencies in the human service field means that other considerations will be the determinants of selection or purchasing, rather than the possession of a relatively static quality assurance system certification.

TOTAL QUALITY MANAGEMENT IN HUMAN SERVICES

All of the above techniques can be seen to be insufficient in themselves to form the basis of an adequate approach to quality in human services, one that covers all the aspects of such services which make them unique and different from other service industries. As a result, in tandem with the approach to quality that stresses the features of the quality assurance system, there has been great interest in human services in developing what could be termed the total quality management (TQM) approach, which we discussed in detail earlier in the book, when reviewing the main features of this approach.

There are a number of reasons why such an approach should have a usefulness for human services, and should be beneficial. Firstly, as we have seen before, most human services are based on a set of values or principles that need to be communicated to all staff if they are to be the basis upon which their work is conducted. TQM is very much to do with values, and the culture of the service that results from the implementation of these values in practice. Secondly, human services are more concerned with the "soft" aspects of quality, and as such are eminently suitable for the interpersonal approach that TQM espouses, rather than the "hard" techniques of many industrial quality assurance systems. Thirdly, because consumers are a vital part of the service delivery process, and are at the heart of human services, a TQM approach that stresses the involvement and participation of consumers should be beneficial. Fourthly, most human services rely greatly on the competence and professional skills of the people delivering them, with less reliance on formal working procedures. TQM stresses the need for the individuals to be committed to a quality approach, and to be the main element in its implementation.

Despite the attractiveness of TQM in human services, outside the health field there are few published accounts of its use, although many advocate its use in a variety of settings and with many client groups (see Dickens, 1991, for example), and the written work tends to be exhortatory in nature. TQM is suggested as the answer to quality problems in many human service settings, including education (Ivancevich and Ivancevich, 1992), government services in general (Swiss, 1992), health care (Fried, 1992), services for people with disabilities (ACDD, 1993) and higher education (Edwards, 1991). There is a series of texts written by Hugh Koch intended for health services (1992, 1993), public services in general (1991) and mental health services (1991). We will examine this latter work later in the chapter.

TQM in Health Care

One important contributor in the field of TQM applied to health care is Donald Berwick, whose writings combine the exhortatory approach mentioned above with practical advice based on the experience gained in setting up and running TQM schemes in acute hospitals (Berwick, 1992; Berwick, Godfrey and Roessner, 1990; Berwick, Enthoven and Bunker, 1992). Berwick criticises current quality assurance practices in health care for concentrating purely on the control aspects of quality, such as clinical audit, and neglecting an overall approach. He writes:

> Do not rely on audit to achieve improvement. Rely, instead, on an overall system of improvement within which audit has a limited, albeit necessary, role. (Berwick, 1992, p. 3)

He defines a "system of improvement" as a set of guiding principles through which the work of individuals can contribute to the improvement of health care as a whole. TQM offers a way of linking the work of the individual to the benefit of the whole organisation. He sets out eight principles of a system of improvement, that are close to many of the principles of TQM mentioned in the last chapter. They are:

1. *Intention to change.* For any organisation to improve there must be an intention to do so. Traditional audit-based systems do not address this, but merely constitute an inspection system that registers whether a care process meets some arbitrary level of acceptability.

2. *Definition of quality.* Each organisation must define quality for itself, and in a way that represents the needs of its customers. In health care Berwick says that this can be done by listing the results and attributes of the health care system that are wanted by the people who depend on that system. He cautions against ambiguity in defining quality, so that there can be clarity of purpose.

3. *Measurement of quality.* To maintain continuous improvement, any system of quality requires constant measurement, as this is the only way to gauge success or change. In addition it is necessary to use statistical techniques to analyse, interpret and present the data for their best use. Information is required on the patients, the staff, resources (material and financial), care processes, and on the organisation as a system.

4. *Understanding interdependence.* In health care, effective improvement requires a comprehension of, and working with, the health care system as a whole. Concentration on one aspect of it—for example the delivery of professional care as monitored by clinical audit—ignores the contribution to the quality of the health care system as a whole of other professions and support services.

5. *Understanding systems.* This principle underlies the previous one, and suggests that effective improvement depends far more on better systems than on other factors such as material rewards and incentives. Problems when they occur are problems of the system, and not of individuals, and so continuous improvement must concentrate on systemic change rather than individual change alone.

6. *Investment in learning.* A continually improving organisation is one that continually learns. This learning is not only in terms of better care practices, or increased individual competence, but also in terms of organisational and systemic effectiveness.

7. *Reduction in costs.* Effective improvement efforts seek systematically to reduce waste, duplication, unnecessary complexity and unwanted variation. Improving quality and saving money can

be done at the same time and, usually, the former leads to the latter. This again requires a focus on the health care system as a whole, and on reducing organisational costs rather than individual costs.

8. *Leadership commitment*. Improvement requires leadership, and also action by leaders. Leadership not only has symbolic effects, it demonstrates to the whole organisation that there is an environment of continual improvement.

A major contribution to the debate on health care quality and the use of TQM techniques is the review by Claus (1991). She reviewed five models of TQM in current use in the United States. Drawing on these models, Claus constructs a further model that uses the main elements of each system and adds more; seen as important in the TQM process to build a model which is eclectic and comprehensive. TQM is seen as a model of organisational change, with continuous improvement as its goal. In order to accomplish this, the environment of the hospital or health care setting will need to become a learning organisation, and a number of change steps or phases need to be undertaken. The five phases are described below.

Phase one—organising for change entails activities such as assessment of the present situation, development of leadership, planning of the change process and goal setting.

Phase two—preparing the hospital environment means a number of preparatory activities such as information-giving, creation of an awareness of quality issues, development of customer orientation and obtaining a commitment to quality improvement.

Phase three—empowering the employees requires that teams and individuals are given responsibility for change and improvement.

Phase four—focusing the hospital environment means that small changes are instituted so that they become the focus of activity, and beneficial improvements are seen to happen. These small changes require to be related to the overall plan and reviewed where necessary.

Phase five—engaging the hospital environment requires that the change is institutionalised within the structure and culture of the hospital. Two conditions need to be present for this to happen: evidence of staying power and achieved outcomes.

In order to be effective, the TQM programme must be developed in a careful, coordinated and time-phased way, so that eventually it will be both integrated and comprehensive in its effects and process. Claus outlines a three-phase model that is in turn divided into discrete actions for implementation.

Phase one—executive education and commitment focuses on senior management and consists of three steps: assessment of present quality activities and information gathering related to strategic planning, management styles, quality measures and customer requirements; planning of the introduction of TQM and the needs of the organisation based on the assessment carried out; an executive retreat to increase awareness and commitment, to develop a consensus view of quality and to agree the implementation plan for TQM.

Phase two—middle management/supervisory education and action is geared at the middle management level and again is divided into three steps: awareness and commitment, where the quality action plans are translated in objectives of this level and the gaining of commitment to change; vertical task force education, where cross-disciplinary task forces are set up to develop the quality plans and measures for subsections of the organisation; advanced TQM training in the tools and techniques of quality, and how to apply them in a health care context.

Phase three—all employee education and action is geared to all the employees and includes three steps: awareness and commitment which must be communicated from the higher levels; quality education and training, particularly in problem-solving techniques and the TQM process; quality action, where all employees participate in continuous improvement processes in a variety of ways.

Throughout these phases Claus describes six key processes that are at work, and which help define TQM in health care: assessment, measurement, ongoing employee education, communications and feedback, system information and tracking, and recognition/ reward.

Problems of TQM in Human Services

Claus lists the ultimate benefit of TQM as "meeting customers' expectations at lower cost", but she also reviews four possible obstacles to the implementation of TQM in a health care setting, that have to be tackled if this implementation is to succeed. These are, firstly, the heavy reliance in health care systems on one aspect of a quality system—the quality assurance mode—which is mainly limited to inspection functions rather than improvement functions, the meeting of requirements rather than expectations, and focuses on monitoring rather than improvement. Secondly, the professional dominance of the medical profession and their emphasis on personal autonomy can impede the development of true teamwork. Thirdly, resistance can be encountered from the many other professional interests that operate in health care settings, and which are often motivated by professional self-interest rather than corporate development. Lastly, the difficult financial situation of most health care organisations, in both the United States and Britain, may deprive the TQM process of the necessary resources to ensure successful implementation.

Others have criticised an unquestioning approach to TQM in health care settings. Smith (1992) conducted a two-year study of 59 hospitals and compared these to a similar number of business organisations, in terms of the implementation of TQM. She concludes that traditional TQM approaches are not ideal for health care applications. For example, professional staff were found to spend a third of their time in handling operational problems in TQM caused by poor clerical and communications activities. Similarly Mueller (1992) writes that any successful implementation of TQM in health care must recognise some crucial differences between health care and other service industry settings. These include five key differences:

1. Health care workers are, on the whole, professionals.

2. The nature of the work they do is very different, involving human life.

3. It is difficult to measure the health care process.

4. Typical TQM jargon is inappropriate in health care settings.

5. Adversarial relationships often exist between management and health care professionals.

Answers to these problems lie in careful consideration of TQM systems and their implementation. Godfrey, Berwick and Roessner

(1992) report a number of lessons learnt from early implementations of TQM in the United States:

1. Effective quality management begins at the top, or at least is owned by the top as soon as it begins.

2. Any health care organisation that begins a major TQM initiative without the involvement of doctors does so at its peril.

3. What works well in one health care organisation might not work well in another. Each organisation has to create a quality management structure in its own image and likeness.

4. Unless quality improvements are informed and guided by a general theory, they will have a tendency to become self-serving, and focus on the internal needs of professionals rather than the external needs of customers.

In a British setting Natrass (1992), from experience of implementing a TQM approach in an English health authority, suggests similar points, including the difficulty of implementing TQM, the need to develop leadership in all levels of the organisation at the same time, and the need for that leadership to be active in, and committed to, quality in all aspects of the job.

There is a real danger that, as in industry, two contradictory responses will occur in health care services concerning TQM. The first is the "bandwagon" effect, where many organisations jump on the TQM roller-coaster, seeing it as the answer to all their service problems, without considering points like those raised above. The second is the dismissal of TQM as unnecessary if other quality initiatives are in place, such as BS5750/ISO9000 or clinical audit procedures. TQM involves these initiatives within a total framework of quality improvement, as well as being concerned with interpersonal processes, and the core attitudes and values of the service. This latter point is summed up by Maxwell (1992) revisiting his dimensions of quality that we discussed in Chapter 3, as one of his "eight laws of implementing quality":

1. Commitment to quality for those served.

2. Translation of good ideas into action, usually by persistent small steps and testing against external indicators of performance.

3. Emphasis on team performance.

4. Systematic elimination of waste, flaws in performance and barriers to good performance.

5. Recognition of every staff member's dual responsibility, that is, to do the job well and find ways of doing it better.

6. Diagnostic use of quality concepts (for example the six dimensions [q.v.]) to determine when to intervene to raise quality.

7. Continual measurement of progress in order to support improvement.

8. Viewing particular quality initiatives within the broader context of quality in the system as a whole.

TQM in Mental Health

Despite the rapid increase in attempts to implement TQM in acute medical settings, particularly in the United States, there are few recorded attempts to do the same with the other client groups we have featured in our examples in this and the previous chapter, and which represent the major work areas of most clinical psychologists. The Accreditation Council on Services for People with Developmental Disabilities in the United States has recently espoused the use of TQM (ACDD, 1993) in such services, and many of the descriptions of quality assurance systems in Bradley and Bersani (1990) could be considered as descriptions of TQM programmes, although the label is not used.

Rago and Reid (1991) describe a TQM programme set up in a psychiatric hospital in Texas. Five concepts of quality formed the basis of this implementation, summed up as: total, quality, customer, work flow process, and empowerment. Two examples are given, one stressing the total hospital environment and identifying four levels of action that were used, involving a quality improvement council, a performance evaluation team, the establishment of performance goals and a front line quality improvement team. The second example looked at TQM at a unit level, involving self-managing teams, work flow process analysis in psychological treatment and strategies for team empowerment. Quality tools employed included nominal group technique, statistical process control and Pareto analysis. The crucial aspect in their report is the realisation that the quality of a service is determined by the workers who deliver it.

A thorough approach to TQM in mental health, and a guide for its implementation, has been produced by Hugh Koch as part of a series of publications on TQM in public services and health services. Building on his comprehensive approach to TQM in health care (1991, 1992), Koch outlines a model of TQM in mental health services and a plan for its implementation. He introduces TQM as:

> An approach which comprehensively introduces quality techniques, systems and culture into a service in such a way that all departments, units or staff groups are involved. It implies that the quality process must be managed and coordinated, rather than relying on people's professionalism or personal maturity. (Koch, 1991, p. 1)

After defining quality in terms of Maxwell's six dimensions, he thinks that there are five aspects of TQM in mental health services:

1. Putting the service user (and carers) first.
2. Being fully aware of the service users' expectations and needs.
3. Satisfying service users, whenever possible, first time.
4. Recognising and reducing the costs of poor quality.
5. Supporting and encouraging individual members of staff and the teams they belong to.

The key practical aspects of the model used by Koch can be summed up in a diagram, seen in Figure 4.

The elements represented in this diagram are:

1. *Standard setting and monitoring.*
2. *Service user information and feedback.* This includes both giving out information on services and asking users for their views concerning satisfaction with the service.
3. *Service user/customer care.* Users must be treated positively and with respect, with high quality customer care and the provision of services tailored to users' needs.

TQM FRAMEWORK

Figure 4   Koch's TQM framework for mental health. Reproduced by permission of the author and Pavilion Publishing (Brighton) Ltd from H.C.H. Koch (1991), *Exceeding Expectations: Total Quality Management in Mental Health Services*, Hove: Pavilion Publishing.

4. *Training*. In the methods of maintaining, monitoring and improving quality.

5. *Clinical audit*. Professional quality is improved through clinical and management audit.

6. *Communication*. This is an important element in empowering staff, both as individuals and as teams, and a way of recognising their value and worth.

7. *Physical environment*. This involves auditing and improving the quality of the physical environment in which care is delivered.

8. *Resource management*. This is the quality cost element, and involves linking quality, costs and resources into the resource management approach.

Over and above all of this is the development of a management culture that places TQM at the forefront of service delivery, and addresses the issue of staff attitudes and values, as well as commitment to quality.

Koch's model is one of very few that are developed fully in the context of mental health services, or indeed any other human service other than health care. As can be seen, it is based heavily on a user's perspective on services, and on the importance of the interpersonal processes involved in service delivery. It also stresses the incorporation of tools and techniques of human service quality, such as clinical audit, into a framework of total quality. Koch assumes the benefits to be improved casework and care, reduction of errors, improved cost effectiveness, improved staff confidence and increased consumer satisfaction with services. Like most descriptions of TQM, these benefits have yet to be shown in research.

TQM—a Possible Further Model for the Therapeutic Professions

Earlier in the book we remarked on the separation between models of quality assurance—and TQM—that have their origins in mainstream industry, and those that arise from human service settings. One of the stated aims of this book is to bring about a "rapprochement" between the two approaches, and in this context, the last part of this chapter is concerned with extending the useful framework for TQM formulated by Dale and Boaden, that was discussed earlier, to human services, particularly the therapeutic professions. Their attempt at providing an integrated "quality improvement framework" appears in diagrammatic form in Figure 3, and it is used here as a useful and practical way of considering the issue of developing a total approach to quality in therapeutic professions, which, as we indicated in the last chapter, suffers from a mainly piecemeal approach.

There are four major sections to the model proposed by Boaden and Dale.

1. *Organising*

    The main characteristic of the model is the need for a formal organised framework for the development of a quality assurance system. The use of such a framework as BS5750/ISO9000 stresses this essential characteristic of an adequate system. In order to develop such an approach within a therapeutic profession, there are a number of actions necessary:

(a) A clear long-term strategy for the quality improvement process must be formulated by all concerned, and integrated with other service policies and activities and with purchasers and other external requirements and policies. The collegiate nature of therapeutic professions should ensure that this process involves active participation by all therapists in the service, and good communication of all aspects to relevant people and agencies. This stage should also involve the development of quality improvement plans and objectives that are more detailed and against which performance could be judged.

(b) A common definition of quality in the therapeutic professions should be formulated or adopted, and specific issues about the TQM process, and its definition, should be discussed.

(c) All sources of potential advice and guidance should be identified. In the therapeutic professions this stage would involve identifying all material that impinges upon the delivery of such services. This will include professional information—such as codes of practice, guidelines for professional practice, and statements of standards of practice and ethics. It will also include the identification of local and national sources of information, such as the national and local Patients' Charter, legislation and authority policies, particularly those mandated by contractors. At this stage the consideration of the need for BS5750/ISO9000 should be discussed.

(d) Formal project planning techniques could be used to identify the necessary stages and actions required to meet the objectives as set out.

(e) All staff should be involved, and their cooperation and participation ensured. At this stage the therapy service's management relationships should be considered, and the legitimacy of taking such an approach to quality should be discussed with the organisation within which the service operates.

(f) A formal programme of education and training in quality issues—both the quality system operation, and the quality aspects of the therapy service such as good practice in procedures and techniques—should be implemented.

(g) An organisational infrastructure that will support, develop, facilitate and maintain the quality approach should be developed and established. This might involve structuring meetings and service activities so that quality issues are regularly discussed. This could be done by setting aside time at regular meetings for such discussion, or scheduling meetings dedicated to such activities as clinical audit and the dissemination of good practice.

2. *Systems and techniques*

This area of the model is concerned with the development of a framework within which quality improvement works, and the application of the "hard" tools and techniques to facilitate this. Actions required in this area by a therapeutic service might include:

(a) Identification of the appropriate tools and techniques of quality assurance. The earlier chapter on such tools and techniques used in the industrial and service industry sector might be useful in the consideration of this, as will the examination of such tools and techniques in human services. This stage might require decisions at a general level—for example the selection of a framework for clinical audit—or at a specific level—the decision on the items in a patient satisfaction measure.

(b) Once the methodology has been arrived at, training is needed in the use of the relevant tools and techniques.

(c) The need for a formal quality system such as BS5750/ISO9000 should be considered and, if it is decided upon, the necessary requirements should be met, in line with the potential interpretation suggested above, or with one which is arrived at locally.

3. *Measurement and feedback*

In this area of the model the needs and requirements of the service purchaser or consumer—clients of various types—will be translated into measures of performance. Actions required from a therapeutic professions viewpoint might include:

(a) Identifying key internal and external performance measures. This will enlarge upon the decisions made in the last area of the model and will also include the process of standard setting for all activity areas.

(b) The expectations and needs and demands of all relevant service stakeholders should be identified. This will include the contractual requirements of service purchasers under contracts let, the views of referring agencies and others, and the direct clients of the service themselves.

(c) Best practice in all aspects of the therapy service's operation and activity should be identified. This may be done by research and ensuring that all procedures and techniques used are up-to-date and reflect the outcome of rigorous experiment. It might also involve "benchmarking"—examining the performance of other relevant services or organisations and identifying the best practice available for specific areas of activity.

(d) Deciding on the means for the communication and celebration of success in meeting quality improvement targets, and recognising individual and team efforts. A reporting system should be established so that feedback is given to staff of the service, purchasers and clients, in forms that are relevant and understandable.

4. *Changing the culture*

Cultural change is an essential aspect in the successful implementation of TQM. As a result actions in this area might include:

(a) Therapists must see the relevance of using a structured approach to quality assurance in their work, and take individual responsibility for the quality of their interactions with clients and others in the work of the service.

(b) There should be an emphasis on the development of people within the organisation, in both skill and personal areas.

(c) The establishment of roles and relationships in respect of teamwork is important, as there are many areas of quality in which the actions of others—other disciplines, professions, family members, etc.—impinge on the work of the therapeutic professions. These factors must be taken into account. Potential areas for interdisciplinary cooperation on quality should be developed, perhaps including multidisciplinary clinical audit, based on multidisciplinary standards in relevant areas. Conflict with others should be minimised, as it detracts from quality.

(d) Performance indicators for the success of the quality approach should be developed, in the same way as performance indicators for the service itself will be established.

There are six practical steps that should be taken in implementing this model (or any similar one) in therapeutic profession services:

1. The service's present position regarding quality should be established, including current measures and performance indicators and service development mechanisms. It might help to produce a "quality map" which locates the service in the context of national, local and internal quality initiatives of every sort to date.

2. Consider the framework described above—or any other one that is relevant—and customise it to suit the service concerned.

3. Assess the features of the service against the framework to see which aspects of it are already in place, and which ones require development.

4. Prioritise the development of features not in place, in line with the priorities of purchasers and the availability of time and financial resources to develop the model.

5. Develop specific plans to introduce the priority features into the service.

6. Identify potential quality problems and develop some solutions to deal with them.

The Elements of a Total Approach to Quality in the Therapeutic Professions

Whether a therapeutic profession service or department decides on a particular approach to quality or not, there are some basic core elements that seem to be essential if the profession is to develop adequate responses to the demands placed on it for quality services by purchasers and consumers. These elements also represent the amalgamation of good practice in quality that has been discussed in all the preceding chapters. In this last section we will list these elements so that they can be considered in the light of the potential frameworks suggested above. They are not listed in any order of priority—this will depend on individual service circumstances.

1. A documented formal framework for quality assurance and management that is agreed with staff and the organisation within which the service is located. This may or may not involve the use of BS5750/ISO9000, depending on the relevance of the possession of that standard to the service and its contractors. The documentation should include descriptions of all the aspects of the approach of the service or department to quality, and might take the form of a quality manual.

2. A set of performance indicators that give basic information on the performance of the service in relevant and pertinent aspects of service provision.

3. The use of techniques and tools of quality that are relevant, and might include:

   (a) Statistical analysis of performance as measured by performance indicators.

   (b) The systematic and programmed use of analytic techniques such as clinical audit and service evaluation.

   (c) The use of reliable and valid measures of service performance such as psychometric tests and process and outcome measures that meet these criteria.

4. The consideration of the best ways of regularly involving clients in the judgement of service quality, bearing in mind the research on consumer satisfaction and its measurement.

5. The consideration of methods for developing staff skills and competence, and ensuring the identification and use of "best practice" in all aspects of the service's activities.

6. Adherence to all relevant codes of practice, guidelines for professional activities and local and national policies and legislation concerning relevant aspects of professional practice.

7. The consideration of values and ethics, both of the service itself and of individual therapists.

8. The development of a set of standards for the performance of the service in all relevant aspects, bearing in mind national and local standards of performance, and the measurement of the service delivery against those standards.

9. The development of an atmosphere for quality—a non-competitive, collegiate ethos, where good practice is valued, and there is recognition of the need for constant improvement at a personal and department or service level.

These elements—and others—should form the basis of any discussion of quality within the therapeutic professions. It is not the intention of this book to be prescriptive about quality or to endorse any particular approach. The present author, however, believes that the field of quality in industry, in service industries and in human services has much to offer by way of indication. This book is an attempt to provide such indication, which may or may not be followed by the therapeutic professions depending on circumstance and motivation. The basic message of the book is that quality assurance within the therapeutic professions should be the subject of a comprehensive, systematic and documented approach.

CHAPTER 9   Epilogue: In pursuit of quality and excellence in human services

ISSUES CONCERNING QUALITY

In this final chapter we will explore briefly some of the issues concerning quality in human services in general and more particularly in our chosen area of application, the therapeutic professions. The concept of quality in human services is deceptively simple. Reduced to a basic statement it might be something along the lines of:

> Improving the quality of people's lives by the application of quality service methods employed by highly competent staff, in such a way as to meet people's needs and expectations.

The research and literature on quality in manufacturing and service industries that we have reviewed in this book have shown us that, in order for these aims to be met, quality must be tackled in a systematic way and involve all aspects of a service, and this system must be used by a workforce committed to quality. The work referred to has also indicated that, in order to be an effective approach to improving the outcome of service delivery, this quality system must employ various tools and techniques that allow quality to be quantified, and a planned approach to improvement must be implemented.

As we saw in Chapter 3, however, there are features of human services that differentiate them from other service industries, and these features have been recurring issues throughout this book. They form a set of issues that need to be considered when discussing quality in human services, or in implementing any quality assurance system.

Values and Quality

In Chapter 3 we saw how one of the main features of quality in human services concerned the issue of values, both personal values—those held by individuals in the service—and service values—those articulated formally or informally, consciously or unconsciously, by the service. We have also seen that a values-based approach has been a fruitful way in which quality can be viewed, measured and implemented. For any human service to be effective, it must operate on a set of values that have meaning for the clients of the service, and which guide a set of actions on the part of the service that are congruent with them. Service dysfunctions occur when the value systems on which the service operates are either not consciously held by those providing the service, are not acknowledged by the service nor shared by all staff, or are at odds with the needs of the clients.

The work reviewed on total quality management (TQM) suggests that the consideration of the issues of values is not unique to human services. Virtually all approaches to TQM stress the need for a fundamental change in values—and corresponding attitudes—on the part of organisations who implement such an approach. As we saw in Chapter 4, TQM can be seen as a values-driven approach, particularly where service industries and more particularly human services are concerned. The ten dimensions of service quality of Parasuraman, Zeithaml and Berry (1985), as shown in Table 1, are in themselves a set of values concerning the interaction of consumer and service provider. When reduced to their constituent factors—tangibles, reliability, responsiveness, assurance and empathy—they come very close to the dimensions of effectiveness and quality in other human service fields, for example the empathy, warmth and genuineness dimensions of effective psychotherapist performance (Rogers, Gendlin, Kiesler and Truax, 1967). These dimensions were, however, obtained from samples of consumers, and represent their views on the value systems on which services should operate. Many other value systems—such as normalisation—are service-generated systems, and may not be coherent with the views of consumers about the type and quality of service they wish to receive. The values of the service providers, however rational and liberal, may still be at odds with those of the consumer.

One issue about the influence of values on quality concerns the difficulty in synthesising a values-based "soft" approach with a "hard" systematic operational view of quality assurance procedures. Despite the attempts of most systems of TQM to incorporate both types of approach to quality, there is still a need to tackle the issue of measurement and analysis of value issues. If, as we have said, any comprehensive approach to quality management included objective definition and measurement of staff performance, in structure, process and outcome terms, then staff actions that are predominantly an expression of values should be subject to the same processes. Such measurements involve subjective concepts that do not lend themselves easily to reliable and valid measures. How do we measure love? Or dignity? The employment of both values and emotions is a characteristic of many human service systems, but these essential aspects remain outside any known, useful measurement system. We cannot say, for example, that service A is of a higher quality than service B, because the staff in service A show 50% more love towards their clients. Similarly, purchasers and contractors cannot use these variables as the basis on which to choose between providers, despite the fact that the values and emotions, and the extent to which they influence the staff of the service's actions towards clients, might be the crucial difference in service quality. In such instances, it is not surprising that most approaches to quality stick with the easy bits—the Performance Indicators and standards type of approach.

Money and Quality

In human services, virtually any discussion of quality soon turns towards a discussion of money. Many of the approaches to quality assurance, and the tools and techniques of quality in human services, are predicated on money. Performance Indicators exist to provide differentiation for financial allocation amongst agencies by a funding body. Clinical audit allows resource use to be linked to clinical effectiveness, the so-called "resource management" or "clinical budgeting" approach popular in the British National Health Service in the 1980s. The field of health economics attempts to link outcome and cost. It is an inescapable fact, however, that a quality human service is also an efficient one in the use of resources, that is it produces an effective outcome and output in relation to input or resources.

Our review of quality in industry looked at the issue of quality costs. This approach stresses the importance of improving quality through the reduction of faults, and in the use of financial information in feeding back to the workforce the implications of errors and quality problems. In service industries, however, where the tangible product is usually less important, the quality cost concept concerns the aspect of the service delivery process that can influence the future choice of the service by a discerning consumer. Poor quality service is a cost to the organisation in that not only will the consumer not use the organisation again but he or she will also tell others of their bad experience and thus discourage them from using it as well. In human services, as we have seen, the issue of choice is a difficult one, and the informed or discerning consumer, with the power to withhold purchase, is not a relevant concept in that form. Crosby's saying—"quality is free"—may not apply in the same sense under the influence of these factors. Quality systems, as we have seen, need money for their implementation and maintenance; indeed considerable amounts if BS5750/ISO9000 experiences are used as a criterion for assessment. In human services these costs have to be met by funding agencies, who may be subject to financial stringencies, as is the case in most Western countries at the time of writing. There is a real danger that, in pursuit of a pseudo-market economy in human services, quality is seen as an extra, added factor, to be considered only when there is enough money. If, however, we see quality as concerning values, then an emphasis on quality that moves away from costly systems towards a TQM or commitment-based approach would seem to be vital.

Lastly, the preponderance of contracting approaches to human services, of particular relevance to most therapeutic services at present, has led to quality being seen purely in terms of meeting contractual conditions on quality, usually in the form of prescribed standards. This is unfortunate, as it detracts from the values-base of quality as a desirable value in itself, and leads to a rigid standard-setting and -meeting approach where, as we saw in earlier chapters, pursuit of minimal standards eventually becomes the aim of the quality system, rather than an idea of continual improvement.

Systems and Quality

Our review of quality assurance, control and management systems in the manufacturing and service industry, and human services fields, leads to the conclusion that any adequate approach to developing quality services requires the adoption of a systematic approach, perhaps using a model or system to provide a structure or framework on or around which a suitable quality management system can be built. We have looked in this book at models of TQM and at the use of BS5750/ISO9000 as examples of this type of structure or framework, and assessed their suitability in human services, and among the therapeutic professions.

There is a real danger here that the pursuit of a system of quality assurance may lead to a view of quality as being systems-led. The energy, commitment, resources and activity needed to install a system such as BS5750/ISO9000 are considerable, and once it is installed, it demands continual maintenance in order to be retained and developed. Before embarking on the implementation of such a system, some basic questions should be asked concerning suitability and necessity. These issues have been addressed at various points in this book, and the conclusion reached that whilst BS5750/ISO9000 is an important framework and contains valuable guidance for structuring an adequate quality system, it should not be seen as a panacea for all quality ills, to be applied whatever the diagnosis or aetiology of the illness. The advantages and disadvantages of using such a framework should be considered, as well as its relevance to the clients' needs and demands. Could the energy, resources, and so on spent on introducing BS5750/ISO9000 and gaining accreditation be better spent on services or staff of more direct benefit to the clients? Could the desired improvement in quality of service be brought about by simpler, less bureaucratic means? Is the management style of the service suited to using such a managerially-based system, or is it a people-based management style, where such an approach would be anathema? Each organisation must answer such questions for itself.

People and Quality

The work we have reviewed concerning the quality of human services, and of service industries in general, stresses the vital role in quality of the people delivering the service. The key to quality in services, particularly human services, lies in the "moment of truth", the point where service provider and service consumer interact. In human services, the total reason for the existence of the service is usually to provide this "moment of truth" in a way that will benefit the consumers or improve their quality of life. The quality of the human service depends in a large part on the way in which this interaction is handled, and how it then affects the outcome for the consumer.

To a large extent, in human services, this issue concerns the competence of the service staff. This factor in turn is influenced by training, its content and relevance to the work carried out, staff development opportunities, and the commitment of staff to undertaking their work with quality as the main consideration. In the context of most therapeutic professions, the basic training aspect is well covered, as we have seen, with accreditation systems and course reviews. There is little attention paid, however, to staff development in most services. Once qualified, therapists need to remain continually in touch with the literature and good practice.

The attitude and commitment of staff towards quality depends to a large extent upon the management style and leadership shown in the service, and whether this permits involvement and cooperation. It is impossible, as Tom Peters constantly reiterates, to impose an open, people-based commitment to TQM on a rigid hierarchical management structure. The latter must change for the former to be effective. One of the dilemmas of quality is the need to reconcile a structured, planned approach to continual quality improvement with the openness, flexibility and commitment to innovation that the pursuit of quality and excellence demands if it is to be successful.

At the very least, in a quality service, the staff should be treated with the same basic values of dignity, respect and courtesy as they are encouraged to employ with the clients. This requires, as O'Brien (1990) points out, the exercise of real leadership skills and attributes on the part of human service managers. Too often there is exhortation to quality of interaction of staff where the same skills are not modelled in practice by the service managers towards the staff. The development of a total approach to quality demands that all staff are involved, in all aspects of their working life. There is evidence to show that the quality of care received by the clients of human services is directly correlated with the quality of working life experienced by the staff delivering that care (Karan and Mettel, 1989).

The Quality of Life

In this book we have not addressed the issue of quality of life to any great extent. This is not because it is seen as an unimportant topic—indeed the opposite—but because in itself it constitutes a large topic worthy of more discussion than space permits. In most human services, the improvement of the quality of life of the clients is the major goal of the service, and the major outcome for individuals. Various approaches can be taken on its definition, from a socio-philosophical perspective—for example Mukherjee (1989)—to an economic one—for example the QALY (Quality Adjusted Life Years) economic analysis tool (Gudex and Kind, 1988). There is a widespread acceptance that the measurement of quality of life, whilst difficult, is a vital part of quality evaluation and the production and use of adequate outcome measures for human services. Fallowfield (1990) has reviewed a number of measures and approaches in the area of physical well-being, and reports a paradox that faces all who would apply such measures, in that their application detracts from a holistic approach and over-simplifies an issue that is affected as much by factors external to the care process as by those internal to it.

It is obvious that quality of life, and its experience, can only be defined by the client or consumer, and so the use of this concept is linked to the ideas of consumer satisfaction that we have referred to throughout this book. If the goal of a human service is to improve quality of life, then the consumer's judgement of satisfaction with that service will to some extent be a reflection of an improvement in their quality of life status. Some authors have used this approach as the basis for quality measurement systems; see Ager's *Life Experiences Checklist* (1990) for example. A consideration that arises is whether satisfaction with quality of life and, ipso facto, with service quality, is a state or trait. Empirical research (Diener, 1984) suggests that it might be a stable, global trait of positive self-regard, whilst there are also contradictory suggestions (Argyle, 1992) that it might be a combination of positive moods and specific satisfactions, affected by underlying personality characteristics such as introversion–extroversion. Whatever the case may be, there are some essential characteristics of quality of life that have a bearing on the importance of using this, and other, measures of consumer satisfaction as crucial elements in the judgement of service quality. Goode (1990) thinks three premises apply that have such relevance:

1. Quality of life is basically a social phenomenon, and a product of interaction with others—in our case in a human service context.

2. Quality of life is the outcome of individuals fulfilling, or being helped to fulfil, basic human needs, in a way satisfactory to themselves.

3. Quality of life is a matter of consumer rather than professional definition. It concerns how the consumer perceives and evaluates his own situation, rather than how others determine this for them.

In our chosen field of application, it is obvious that the justification for the existence of most therapeutic services is to improve the quality of life of their clients. If they do not do this, then the effectiveness of the outcomes for each individual is suspect, and the services' input useless. Wilde and Svanberg (1990) define quality in one therapeutic profession—clinical psychology—on the basis of quality of life. They conclude:

> The development and use of quality of life measures is therefore central to a proper evaluation of the impact of ... care. Quality of life considerations are likely to constitute an increasingly important set of criteria by which to evaluate the effectiveness of interventions. (Wilde and Svanberg, 1990, p. 5)

Consumer satisfaction is the most important part of any quality system, and the lesson of much of this book is that it is *the* most vital part of any quality management or assurance system. The focus should not be on "Why?", but "How?".

REFERENCES

Abdellah, F.G. and Levine, E. (1957) What patients say about their nursing care. *Hospitals*, **31**: 44–48.

Accreditation Council on Services for People with Developmental Disabilities (1988) *A Manager's Guide to Program Evaluation*, Washington, DC: ACDD.

Accreditation Council on Services for People with Developmental Disabilities (1990) *Standards and Interpretation Guidelines for Services for People with Developmental Disabilities*, Washington, DC: ACDD.

Accreditation Council on Services for People with Developmental Disabilities (1993) More than theory: the problem with total quality management in action. *Update on Quality*, **9**, 3: 1–2.

Ager, A. (1990) *The Life Experiences Checklist*, Windsor: NFER– Nelson.

American Supplier Institute (1987) *Quality Function Deployment*, Washington, DC: American Supplier Institute.

Anderson, J. (1991), User satisfaction, user participation and evaluation of mental health services: Experiences in the USA and Britain. In: *National Perspectives on Quality Assurance in Mental Health Care*, Geneva: World Health Organisation.

Argyle, M. (1992) *The Social Psychology of Everyday Life*, London: Routledge.

Ashbaugh, J.W. (1990) The role of performance contracts in quality assurance. In: Bradley, V.J. and Bersani, H.A. (Eds) *Quality Assurance for Individuals with Developmental Disabilities: It's Everybody's Business*, Baltimore, MD: Paul H. Brookes Publishing.

Barkham, M. (1989) Exploratory therapy in two-plus-one sessions I: A rationale for a brief therapy model. *British Journal of Psychotherapy*, **6**, 1: 81–87.

Barra, R. (1989) *Putting Quality Circles to Work: A Practical Strategy for Boosting Productivity and Profits*, New York, NY: McGraw-Hill.

Barrick, M.R. and Alexander, R.A. (1987) A review of quality circle efficacy and the existence of positive-findings bias. *Personnel Psychology*,
40: 579–592.

Barrick, M.R. and Alexander, R.A. (1992) Estimating the benefits of quality circle intervention. *Journal of Organizational Behaviour*, **13**: 73–80.

Berwick, D.M. (1992) Heal thyself or heal thy system: Can doctors help to
improve medical care? *Quality in Health Care*, **1** supplement: S2–S8.

Berwick, D.M., Enthoven, A. and Bunker, J.P. (1992) Quality management
in the NHS: The doctor's role. *British Medical Journal*, **304**: 235–239.

Berwick, D.M., Godfrey, A. and Roessner, J. (1990) *Curing Health Care*, San
Francisco: Jossey-Bass.

Bible, G.H. and Sneed, T.J. (1976) Some effects of an accreditation survey
on program completion at a state institution. *Mental Retardation*, **14**:
14–15.

Boaden, R.J. and Dale, B.G. (1993) Managing quality improvement in
financial services: A framework and case study. *The Service Industries
Journal*, **13**, 1: 17–39.

Boruch, R.F. and Rindskopf, D. (1984) Data analysis. In: Rutman, L. (Ed.)
Evaluation Research and Methodology: A Basic Guide, London: Sage.

Braddock, D. and Mitchell, D. (1992) *Residential Services and Developmental
Disabilities in the United States*, Washington, DC: American Association
on Mental Retardation.

Bradley, V.J. (1990) Conceptual issues in quality assurance. In: Bradley,
V.J. and Bersani, H.A. (Eds) *Quality Assurance for Individuals with
Developmental Disabilities: It's Everybody's Business*, Baltimore, MD: Paul
H. Brookes Publishing.

Bradley, V.J. and Bersani, H.A. (1990) *Quality Assurance for Individuals with
Developmental Disabilities: It's Everybody's Business*, Baltimore, MD: Paul
H. Brookes Publishing.

Bright, K. and Cooper, C.L. (1993) Organisational culture and the management of quality: Towards a new framework. *Journal of Managerial
Psychology* (in press).

British Standards Institute (1991) *BS5750 part 8: Guide to Quality
Management and System Elements for Services*, Milton Keynes: British
Standards Institute.

Bromsgrove and Redditch Health Authority (1988) *Evaluating a Service for
People with Learning Difficulties*, Redditch: Bromsgrove and Redditch
Health Authority.

Brooks, T. (1992) Success through organisational audit. *Health Services
Management*, **88**, 8: 13–15.

Brown, H. and Smith, H. (1992) *Normalisation: A Reader for the Nineties*,
London: Routledge.

Brown, R.I., Bayer, M.B. and MacFarlane, C. (1988) Quality of life
amongst handicapped people. In: Brown, R.I. (Ed.) *Quality of Life for
Handicapped People*, London: Croom Helm.

Brown, S.W., Gummesson, E., Edvardsson, B. and Gustavsson, B. (1991) *Service Quality: Multidisciplinary and Multinational Perspectives*, Lexington, MA: Lexington Books.

Brunning, H., Cole, C. and Huffington, C. (1990) *The Change Directory*, Leicester: The British Psychological Society Division of Clinical Psychology.

Burchard, S.N., Hasazi, J.E. and Gordon, L.R. (1989) *Quality of life in community residential alternatives: results of a three year longitudinal study* (unpub).

Burn, G.R. (1990) Quality function deployment. In: Dale, B.G. and Plunkett, J.J. (Eds) *Managing Quality*, London: Philip Allan.

Campbell, D.T. and Stanley, J.C. (1963) *Experimental and Quasi-experimental Designs for Research*, Chicago, IL: Rand-McNally.

Campbell, D.T., Steenbarger, B.N., Smith, T.W. and Stuckey, R.J. (1982) An ecological systems approach to evaluation. *Evaluation Review*, **6**: 625–648.

Canadian Council on Hospital Accreditation (1985) *Standards for the Accreditation of Canadian Health Care Facilities*, Ottawa: CCHA.

Carman, J. (1990) Consumer perceptions of service quality: An assessment of the SERVQUAL dimensions. *Journal of Retailing*, **66**, 1: 33–55.

Carr-Hill, R., Dixon, P. and Thompson, A. (1989) Too simple for words. *The Health Service Journal*, **99**, 5155: 728–730.

Ceridwen, J. (1992) Using quality's tools: What's working well? *Journal for Quality and Participation*, **15**, 2: 92–99.

Claus, L.M. (1991) Total quality management: A healthcare application. *Total Quality Management*, **2**, 2: 131–148.

Clifford, P., Leiper, R., Lavender, A. and Pilling, S. (1989) *Assuring Quality in Mental Health Services: The QUARTZ System*, London: RDP.

Collard, R. (1989) *Total Quality: Success through People*, London: Institute of Personnel Management.

Committee on Training in Clinical Psychology (1991) *Guidelines for the Assessment of Clinical Psychology Training Courses*, Leicester: The British Psychological Society.

Conroy, J.W. and Bradley, V.J. (1985) *The Pennhurst Longitudinal Study: A Report of Five Years of Research and Analysis*, Boston, MA: Human Services Research Institute.

Conroy, J.W., Walsh, R. and Feinstein, C. (1987) Consumer satisfaction: People with mental retardation moving from institutions to the community. In: S. Breuning and R. Gable (Eds) *Advances in Mental Retardation and Developmental Disabilities*, vol. 3, Greenwich, CT: JAI Press, pp. 135–150.

Cook, T.D. and Campbell, D.T. (1979) *Quasi-experimentation: Design and Analysis for Field Settings*, Chicago, IL: Rand-McNally.

Cormack, D. (1992) Vision to regain lost values. *Professional Manager*, **1**, 1: 16–18.

Coursey, R.D. (1977) Basic questions and tasks. In: Coursey, R.D., Specter, G.A., Murrell, S.A. and Hunt, B. (Eds) *Program Evaluation for Mental Health*, New York, NY: Grune & Stratton.

Coursey, R.D., Specter, G.A., Murrell, S.A. and Hunt, B. (1977) *Program Evaluation for Mental Health: Methods, Strategies and Participants*, New York, NY: Grune & Stratton.

Cronin, J.J. Jnr and Taylor, S.A. (1992) Measuring service quality: A reexamination and extension. *Journal of Marketing*, **56**, July: 55–68.

Crosby, P.B. (1979) *Quality is Free*, New York: McGraw-Hill.

Czepiel, J.A., Solomon, M.R. and Suprenant, C.F. (1985) *The Service Encounter: Managing Employee/Customer Interaction in Service Businesses*, Lexington, MA: Lexington Books.

Dale, B.G. (1986) Experiences with quality circles and quality costs. In: Moores, B. (Ed.) *Are They Being Served?* Oxford: Philip Allan.

Dale, B.G. and Boaden, R.J. (1993) A Total Quality Framework which Works, *TQM Magazine*, **5**,1: 23-26.

Dale, B.G. and Cooper, C.L. (1992) *Total Quality and Human Resources*, Oxford: Blackwell.

Dale, B.G., Lascelles, D.M. and Plunkett, J.J. (1990) The process of total quality management. In: Dale, B.G. and Plunkett, J.J. (Eds) *Managing Quality*, London: Philip Allan.

Dale, B.G. and Plunkett, J.J. (1990) *Managing Quality*, London: Philip Allan.

Dale, B.G. and Plunkett, J.J. (1991) *Quality Costing*, London: Chapman & Hall.

Dalley, G. (1988) *Ideologies of Caring: Rethinking Community and Collectivism*, London: Macmillan.

Dalley, G. (1989) On the road to quality. *The Health Service Journal*, **99**, 5150: 580.

Dalley, G. (1992) Social welfare ideologies and normalisation: Links and conflicts. In: Brown, H. and Smith, H. (Eds) *Normalisation: A Reader for the Nineties*, London: Routledge.

Davidow, W.H. and Uttal, B. (1989) *Total Customer Service*, New York: Harper & Row.

Day, C. (1989) *Taking Action with Indicators*, London: HMSO.

Deming, W.E. (1982) *Quality, Productivity and Competitive Position*, Boston, MA: MIT Press.

Department of Health and Social Security (1971) *Report of the Committee of Enquiry into Conditions in Ely Hospital, Cardiff*, London: HMSO.

Department of Health Social Services Inspectorate (1989) *Homes Are for Living in*, London: HMSO.

Department of Health (1989) *Working for Patients*, London: HMSO.

Dickens, P. (1990) Aiming for excellence in mental handicap services. *International Journal of Health Care Quality Assurance*, **3**, 1: 4–8.

Dickens, P. (1991) "Aiming for Excellence"—the evaluation of quality of life and quality of services for people with a mental handicap. In: *National Perspectives on Quality Assurance in Mental Health Care*, Geneva: World Health Organisation.

Dickens, P. and Horne, T. (1991) A quality status symbol. *The Health Service Journal*, **101**, 5269: 25.

Diener, E. (1984) Subjective well-being. *Psychological Bulletin*, **95**: 542–575.

Disney, J. and Bendall, A. (1990) The potential for the application of Taguchi methods of quality control in British industry. In: Dale, B.G. and Plunkett, J.J. (Eds) *Managing Quality*, London: Philip Allan.

Dixon, N. (1989) *A Guide to Medical Audit*, Hereford: National Association of Quality Assurance in Health Care.

Donabedian, A. (1966) Evaluating the quality of medical care. *Millbank Memorial Fund Quarterly*, **44**, 2: 166–206.

Donabedian, A. (1980) *The Definition of Quality and Approaches to its Assessment*, Ann Arbor, MD: Health Administration Press.

Dotchin, J.A. and Oakland, J.S. (1992) Theories and concepts in total quality management. *Total Quality Management*, **3**, 2: 133–145.

Dowson, S. (1991) *Moving to the Dance*—or Service Culture and Community Care, London: Values into Action.

Edwards, D. (1991) Total quality management in higher education. *Management Services*, **35**, 12: 18–20.

Ellis, R. (1988) *Professional Competence and Quality Assurance in the Caring Professions*, London: Chapman & Hall.

Ellis, R. and Whittington, D. (1988) Social skills, competence and quality. In: Ellis, R. (Ed.) *Professional Competence and Quality Assurance in the Caring Professions*, London: Chapman & Hall.

Fallowfield, L. (1990) *The Quality of Life: The Missing Measurement in Health Care*, London: Souvenir Press.

Felce, D. (1986) Evaluation by direct observation. In: Beswick, J., Zadik, T. and Felce, D. (Eds) *Evaluating Quality of Care*, Kidderminster: British Institute of Mental Handicap.

Fenton-Lewis, A. and Modle, J. (1982) Health indicators: What are they? An approach to efficacy in health care. *Health Trends*, **14**: 3–8.

Fenwick, A.C. (1991) Five easy lessons: A primer for starting a total quality management program. *Quality Progress*, **24**: 63–66.

Fine, C.H. (1985) *Managing Quality: A Comparative Assessment*, New York, NY: Booz, Allen & Hamilton.

Flynn, M.C. (1986) Adults who are mentally handicapped as consumers: Issues and guidelines for interviewing. *Journal of Mental Deficiency Research*, **30**: 396–377.

Flynn, M.C. and Saleem, J.K. (1986) Adults who are mentally handicapped and living with their parents: Satisfaction and perceptions regarding their lives and circumstances. *Journal of Mental Deficiency Research*, **30**: 379–387.

Flynn, R.J. (1980) Normalisation, PASS and service quality assessment: How normalising are current human services? In: Flynn, R.J. and Nitsch, K.E. (Eds) *Normalisation, Social Integration and Community Services*, Baltimore, MD: University Park Press.

Fonagy, P. and Higgitt, A. (1989) Evaluating the performance of departments of psychotherapy. *Psychoanalytic Psychotherapy*, **4**, 2: 121–153.

Fried, R.A. (1992) A crisis in health care. *Quality Progress*, **25**, 4: 67–69.

Gardner, J.F. and Parsons, C.E. (1990) Accreditation as synthesis. In: Bradley, V.J. and Bersani, H.A. (Eds) *Quality Assurance for Individuals with Developmental Disabilities: It's Everybody's Business*, Baltimore, MD: Paul H. Brookes Publishing.

Georgiades, N.J. and Phillimore, L. (1975) The myth of the hero innovator and alternative strategies for organisational change. In: Kiernan, C.C. and Woodford, F.P. (Eds) *Behaviour Modification with the Severely Retarded*, London: Associated Scientific Publishers.

Godfrey, A., Berwick, D.M. and Roessner, J. (1992) Can quality management really work in health care? *Quality Progress*, **25**, 4: 23–27.

Goldsmith, W. and Clutterbuck, D. (1984) *The Winning Streak*, London: Weidenfeld & Nicholson.

Goldstone, L. and Illsley, V. (1986) Measuring the quality of nursing care—the Monitor experience. In: Moores, B. (Ed.) *Are They Being Served?* Oxford: Philip Allan.

Goode, D.A. (1990) Thinking about and discussing quality of life. In: Schalock, R.L. (Ed.) *Quality of Life: Perspectives and Issues*, Washington, DC: American Association on Mental Retardation.

Gronroos, C. (1988) Service quality: The six criteria of good perceived service quality. *Review of Business*, **9**, 3: 10–13.

Gudex, C. and Kind, P. (1988) *The QALY Toolkit*, York: Centre for Health Economics.

Hall, T.J. (1992) *The Quality Manual: The Application of BS5750/ISO9000*, Chichester: John Wiley.

Harman, D. and Martin, G. (1992) Managers and medical audit. *Health Services Management*, **88**, 2: 27–29.

Haug, M. and Sussman, M. (1969) Professional autonomy and the revolt of the client. *Social Problems*, **17**: 153–161.

Heller, R. (1993) TQM: Not a panacea but a pilgrimage. *Management Today*, January: 37–40.

Hemp, R. and Braddock, D. (1990) Accreditation of developmental disabilities programs. In: Bradley, V.J. and Bersani, H.A. (Eds) *Quality Assurance for Individuals with Developmental Disabilities: It's Everybody's Business*, Baltimore, MD: Paul H. Brookes Publishing.

Heron, J. (1979) *Peer Review Audit: Collected Papers*, London: British Postgraduate Medical Foundation.

Hollander, R. (1980) A new service ideology: The third mental health revolution. *Professional Psychology: Research and Practice*, **11**, 5: 11–516.

Howell, H., James, J. and Abbott, K. (1990) Quality matters 4: "Ideas into action": The benefits of monitoring through a quality action group. *Mental Handicap*, **18**, 3: 118–124.

Huczynski, A.A. (1993) *Management Gurus: What Makes Them and How to Become One*, London: Routledge.

Hurst, K. and Ball, J. (1990) Service with a smile. *The Health Service Journal*, **100**, 5185: 120–121.

Hutchins, D.H. (1985) *Quality Circles Handbook*, London: Pitman.

Illich, I. (1976) *Limits to Medicine: Medical Nemesis and the Exploration of Health*, London: Marion Boyars.

Illich, I. (1987) *Disabling Professions*, London: Marion Boyars.

Independent Development Council (1986) *Pursuing Quality*, London: Independent Development Council for People with Mental Handicap.

Ishikawa, K. (1985) *What is Total Quality Control?*—the Japanese Way, Englewood Cliffs, NJ: Prentice-Hall.

Ivancevich, D.M. and Ivancevich, S.H. (1992) TQM in the classroom. *Management Accounting*, **74**, 4: 14–15.

Juran, J.M. (1988) *Quality Control Handbook*, New York: McGraw-Hill.

Kano, N., Seraku, N., Takahashi, F. and Tsuji, S. (1984) Attractive quality and must-be quality. *Journal of the Japanese Society for Quality Control*, **14**, 2: 39–48.

Karan, O.C. and Mettel, L. (1989) Training needs in integrated settings. In: Kiernan, W.E. and Schalock, R.L. (Eds) *Economics, Industry and Disability*, Baltimore, MD: Paul H. Brookes Publishing.

Kimmich, M.H. (1990) The South Carolina model. In: Bradley, V.J. and Bersani, H.A. (Eds) *Quality Assurance for Individuals with Developmental Disabilities: It's Everybody's Business*, Baltimore, MD: Paul H. Brookes Publishing.

King, R.D., Raynes, N.V. and Tizard, J. (1971) *Patterns of Residential Care: Sociological Studies in Institutions for Handicapped Children*, London: Routledge & Kegan Paul.

Kiresuk, T.J. and Sherman, R.E. (1968) Goal Attainment Scaling: A general method for evaluating comprehensive community mental health programs. *Community Mental Health Journal*, **4**: 443–453.

Koch, H.C.H. (1991) *Total Quality Management in Public Services*, Hove: Pavilion Publishing.

Koch, H.C.H. (1991) *Exceeding Expectations: Total Quality Management in Mental Health Services*, Hove: Pavilion Publishing.

Koch, H.C.H. (1991) *Total Quality Management in Health Care*, London: Longman.

Koch, H.C.H. (1992) *Implementing and Sustaining TQM in Health Care*, London: Longman.

Koch, H.C.H. (1993) *Making TQM Work in Health Care*, Hove: Pavilion Publishing.

Landesman, S. (1987) The changing structure and function of institutions: The search for optimal group care environments. In: Landesman, S., Vietze, P. and Begab, M. (Eds) *Living Environments and Mental Retardation*, Washington, DC: American Association on Mental Retardation.

Lavender, A. (1987) The measurement of the quality of care in psychiatric rehabilitation settings: Development of the model standards questionnaires. *Behavioural Psychotherapy*, **15**, 3: 201–214.

LeBow, J. (1982) Consumer satisfaction with mental health treatment. *Psychological Bulletin*, **91**, 2: 244–259.

Lees, J. and Dale, B.G. (1990) The development of quality circles. In: Dale, B.G. and Plunkett, J.J. (Eds) *Managing Quality*, London: Philip Allan.

Lehtinen, U. and Lehtinen, J.R. (1991) Two approaches and service quality dimensions. *The Service Industries Journal*, **11**, 3: 287–303.

Lewis, B.R. (1989) Quality in the service sector: A review. *International Journal of Bank Marketing*, **7**: 4–12.

Lindley, P. and Wainwright, A. (1992) Normalisation training: Conversion or commitment? In: Brown, H. and Smith, H. (Eds) *Normalisation: A Reader for the Nineties*, London: Routledge.

Lottman, M.S. (1990) Quality assurance and the courts. In: Bradley, V.J. and Bersani, H.A. (Eds) *Quality Assurance for Individuals with Developmental Disabilities: It's Everybody's Business*, Baltimore, MD: Paul H. Brookes Publishing.

Management Advisory Service (1989) *Review of Clinical Psychology Services*, Cheltenham: Management Advisory Service.

Mansell, J. (1986) The nature of quality assurance. In: Beswick, J., Zadik, T. and Felce, D. (Eds) *Evaluating Quality of Care*, Kidderminster: British Institute of Mental Handicap.

Marinker, M. (1990) *Medical Audit and General Practice*, London: The British Medical Journal.

Maxwell, R.J. (1984) Quality assessment in health. *British Medical Journal*, **12**, 5: 84–86.

Maxwell, R.J. (1992) Dimensions of quality revisited: From thought to action. *Quality in Health Care*, **1**: 171–177.

McGhee, J. (1987) Professionalised service and disabling help. In: Illich, I. (Ed.) *Disabling Professions*, London: Marion Boyars.

McIver, S. (1991) *Obtaining the Views of Users of Mental Health Services*, London: King's Fund Centre for Health Services Development.

Medical Inspectorate of Mental Health (1987) *Frame of Reference: General Mental Institution, Part I*, Rijswijk, Holland: Medical Inspectorate of Mental Health.

Milne, D. (1987) *Evaluating Mental Health Practice: Methods and Applications*, London: Croom Helm.

Moores, B. (1986) *Are They Being Served?* Oxford: Philip Allan.

Moores, B. and Thompson, A. (1986) What 1357 hospital inpatients think about aspects of their stay in British acute hospitals. *Journal of Advanced Nursing,* **11**: 87–102.

Moos, R. (1974) *Evaluating Treatment Environments,* Chichester: John Wiley.

Morrison, S.J. (1990) Managing quality: A historical review. In: Dale, B.G. and Plunkett, J.J. (Eds) *Managing Quality,* London: Philip Allan.

Mueller, R.A. (1992) Implementing TQM in health care requires adaptation and innovation. *Quality Progress,* **25**, 4: 57–59.

Mukherjee, R. (1989) *The Quality of Life: Valuation in Social Research,* London: Sage.

Mullen, P.M. (1985) Performance indicators—is anything new? *Hospital and Health Services Review,* July: 165–167.

Myers, B.A. (1969) *A Guide to Medical Care Administration: Concepts and Principles,* Washington, DC: American Public Health Association.

Natrass, H. (1992) Total quality management within a health district. *Quality in Health Care,* **1**, Supplement: S9–S11.

Normand, C. (1991) *Clinical Audit in Professions Allied to Medicine and Related Therapy Professions,* Belfast: HHCRU, University of Belfast.

O'Brien, J. (1986) A guide to personal futures planning. In: Bellamy, G.T. and Wilcox, B. (Eds) *A Comprehensive Guide to the Activities Catalog: An Alternative Curriculum for Youths and Adults with Severe Disabilities,* Baltimore, MD: Paul H. Brookes Publishing.

O'Brien, J. (1987) *A Framework for Accomplishment,* Decatur, GA: Responsive Systems Associates.

O'Brien, J. (1990) Developing high quality services for people with developmental disabilities. In: Bradley, V.J. and Bersani, H.A. (Eds) *Quality Assurance for Individuals with Developmental Disabilities: It's Everybody's Business,* Baltimore, MD: Paul H. Brookes Publishing.

Oakland, J.S. (1986) *Statistical Process Control,* London: Heinemann.

Oakland, J.S. (1989) *Total Quality Management,* Oxford: Heinemann Professional Publishing.

Øvretveit, J. (1988) *A Peer Review Process for Improving Service Quality,* Uxbridge: BIOSS, Brunel University.

Øvretveit, J. (1991) Costing quality. *Health Services Management,* **87**, 4: 184–186.

Øvretveit, J. (1991) *Quality Health Services,* Uxbridge: BIOSS, Brunel University.

Øvretveit, J. (1992) *Health Service Quality,* London: Blackwell Scientific Publications.

Packwood, T. (1991) The three faces of medical audit. *The Health Service Journal,* **26**, September: 24–26.

Parasuraman, A., Zeithaml, V.A. and Berry, L.L. (1985) A conceptual model of service quality and its implications for future research. *Journal of Marketing,* **49**: 41–50.

Parasuraman, A., Zeithaml, V.A. and Berry, L.L. (1988) SERVQUAL: A multiple item scale for measuring consumer perceptions of service quality. *Journal of Retailing*, **64**, 1: 12–40.

Parry, G. (1992) Improving psychotherapy services: Applications of research, audit and evaluation. *British Journal of Clinical Psychology*, **31**: 3–19.

Peters, T. (1987) *Thriving on Chaos: Handbook for a Management Revolution*, New York: Alfred A. Knopf.

Peters, T. and Austin, N. (1986) *A Passion for Excellence: The Leadership Difference*, Glasgow: Fontana/Collins.

Peters, T. and Waterman, R.H. (1982) *In Search of Excellence: Lessons from America's Best-run Companies*, New York, NY: Harper & Row.

Pfeffer, N. (1992) Strings attached. *The Health Service Journal*, 102, 5296: 22–23.

Phaneuf, M.C. (1976) *Nursing Audit: Self-regulation in Nursing Practice*, 2nd edn, New York, NY: Appleton-Century-Crofts.

Pilgrim, D. and Treacher, A. (1992) *Clinical Psychology Observed*, London: Routledge.

Pirsig, R.M. (1974) *Zen and the Art of Motorcycle Maintenance*, London: Bodley Head.

Plunkett, J.J. and Dale, B.G. (1990) Quality costing. In: Dale, B.G. and Plunkett, J.J. (Eds) *Managing Quality*, London: Philip Allan.

Posavac, E.J. and Carey, R.G. (1980) *Program Evaluation: Methods and Case Studies*, Englewood Cliffs, NJ: Prentice-Hall.

Rago, W.V. and Reid, W.H. (1991) Total quality management strategies in mental health systems. *Journal of Mental Health Administration*, **18**, 3: 253–263.

Raphael, W. (1974) *Just an Ordinary Patient: A Preliminary Survey of Opinions on Psychiatric Units in General Hospitals*, London: King's Fund Centre.

Rayner, P. and Porter, L.J. (1991) BS5750/ISO9000—the experience of small and medium-sized firms. *International Journal of Quality and Reliability Management*, **8**, 6: 16–28.

Raynes, N.V. (1988) *Annotated Directory of Measures of Environmental Quality*, Manchester: Dept. of Social Policy and Social Work, University of Manchester.

Repp, A.C. and Barton, L.E. (1980) Naturalistic observations of institutionalised retarded persons: A comparison of licensure decisions and behavioural observations. *Journal of Applied Behavior Analysis*, **13**: 333–341.

Richards, H. and Heginbotham, C. (1992) *ENQUIRE: Quality Assurance through Observation of Service Delivery: A Workbook*, 2nd edn, London: King's Fund College.

Robertson, L. (1992) *Quality Assurance for Nurses: A Guide to the Understanding and Implementation of ISO9000 (BS5750) to Nursing Services*, Harlow, Essex: Longman.

Robson, M. (1982) *Quality Circles*, London: Gower.

Robson, M. (1984) *Quality Circles in Action*, London: Gower.

Rogers, C.R., Gendlin, G.T., Kiesler, D.V. and Truax, C.B. (1967) *The Therapeutic Relationship and its Impact: A Study of Psychotherapy with Schizophrenics*, Madison, WI: University of Wisconsin Press.

Rooney, E.M. (1988)A proposed quality system specification for the National Health Service. *Quality Assurance*, **14**: 45–53.

Rosander, A.C. (1990) *The Quest for Quality in Services*, New York, NY: Quality Press.

Rossi, P.H. and Freeman, H.E. (1982) *Evaluation: A Systematic Approach*, London: Sage.

Royal College of Nursing (1981) *Towards Standards*, London: Royal College of Nursing.

Russell, I.T. and Wilson, B.J. (1992) Audit: The Third Clinical Science. *Quality in Health Care*, **1**, 1: 51.

Ryan, J. and Thomas, F. (1987) *The Politics of Mental Handicap*, 2nd edn, Harmondsworth: Penguin Books.

Sale, D. (1990) *Quality Assurance*, Basingstoke, Hants: Macmillan.

Sanders, J.R. (1992) *Evaluating School Programs: An Educator's Guide*, London: Corwin Press.

Schein, E. (1980) *Organisational Psychology*, 3rd edn, Englewood Cliffs, NJ: Prentice-Hall.

Schlegelmilch, B.B., Carman, J. and Moore, S.A. (1992) Choice and perceived quality of US and UK family practitioners. *The Service Industries Journal*, **12**, 2: 263–284.

Schvaneveldt, S.J., Enkawa, T. and Miyakawa, M. (1991) Consumer evaluation perspectives of service quality: Evaluation factors and two-way model of quality. *Total Quality Management*, **2**: 149–161.

Seager, P. (1991) General considerations regarding external independent reviews with a description of the Health Advisory Service for England and Wales. In: *National Perspectives on Quality Assurance in Mental Health Care*, Geneva: World Health Organisation.

Shaw, C.D. (1986) *Introducing Quality Assurance*, London: King's Fund Paper No. 64.

Shaw, C.D. (1991) Specifications for hospital medical audit. *Health Services Management*, **87**, 3: 124–125.

Shaw, P. and Dale, B.G. (1990) Statistical process control. In: Dale, B.G. and Plunkett, J.J. (Eds) *Managing Quality*, London: Philip Allan.

Smith, H. (1988) *Collaboration for Change: Partnership between Service Users, Planners and Managers of Mental Health Services*, London: King's Fund Centre.

Smith, J.L. (1992) TQM in hospitals. *Health Systems Review*, **25**, 3: 24–29.

Smith, S. (1986) *How to Take Part in the Total Quality Revolution: A Management Guide*, London: PA Management Consultants.

Solomon, M.R., Suprenant, C.F., Czepiel, J.A. and Gutman, E.G. (1985) A role theory perspective on dyadic interactions: The service encounter. *Journal of Marketing*, **49**, Winter: 99–111.

St John-Brooks, C. (1993) Blueprint for a gold standard. *Times Educational Supplement Further Education Update*, 19 February: 10–11.

Stecher, B.M. and Davis, W.A. (1987) *How to Focus an Evaluation*, London: Sage.

Stevens, G. and Bennett, J. (1989) Clinical audit—occurrence screening for QA. *Health Services Management*, **85**, 4: 178–182.

Stocking, B. (1989) Setting the standard. *The Health Service Journal*, **99**, 5179: 1470–1472.

Swinson, C. (1992) *Delivering a Quality Service: Preparing for BS5750*, London: The Institute of Chartered Accountants in England and Wales.

Swiss, J.E. (1992) Adapting total quality management to government. *Public Administration Review*, **52**, 4: 356–362.

Taguchi, G. (1986) *Introduction to Quality Engineering*, New York: Asian Productivity Organisation.

Thompson, A. (1986) What the patient thinks. In: Moores, B. (Ed.) *Are They Being Served?* Oxford: Philip Allan.

Twain, D. (1975) Developing and implementing a research strategy. In: Streuning, E. and Guttentag, M. (Eds) *Handbook of Evaluation Research*, London: Sage.

Vuori, H.V. (1982) *Quality Assurance of Health Services: Concepts and Methodologies*, 16th edn, Geneva: World Health Organisation.

Walker, T. (1992) Creating total quality improvement that lasts. *National Productivity Review*, **11**: 473–478.

Wandelt, M.A. and Ager, J.W. (1974) *Quality Patient Care Scale*, New York: Appleton-Century-Crofts.

Weinstein, R.M. (1979) Patient attitudes towards mental hospitalisation: A review of quantitative research. *Journal of Health and Social Behaviour*, **20**: 237–258.

Wells, K. and Biegel, D.E. (1991) *Family Preservation Services: Research and Evaluation*, London: Sage.

Whates, P.D., Birzgalis, A.R. and Irving, M. (1982) Accuracy of hospital activity analysis codes. *British Medical Journal*, **274**: 1857–1858.

Whittaker, A., Gardner, S. and Kershaw, J. (1991) *Service Evaluation by People with Learning Difficulties*, London: The King's Fund.

Whittington, D. (1989) Some attitudes to BS5750: A study. *International Journal of Quality and Reliability Management*, **6**, 3: 54–58.

Wilde, E.D. and Svanberg, P.O. (1990) Never mind the width—measure the quality. *Clinical Psychology Forum* No. 30: 2–5.

Williams, P. (1992) *Evaluation of the NIMROD Project with PASS*, Trowbridge: CMHERA.

Williamson, C. (1992) *Whose Standards? Consumer and Professional Standards in Health Care*, Buckingham: Open University Press.

Williamson, J. (1991) Providing quality care. *Health Services Management*, **87**, 1: 18–23.

Wilson, C. (1987) *Hospital-Wide Quality Assurance*, Eastbourne: W.B. Saunders.

Wolfensberger, W. (1972) *The Principle of Normalisation in Human Services*, Toronto: G. Allan Roeher Institute.

Wolfensberger, W. (1983) Social role valorisation: A proposed new term for the principle of normalisation. *Mental Retardation*, **21**: 234–239.

Wolfensberger, W. (1987) Values in the funding of services. *American Journal of Mental Retardation*, **92**: 141–143.

Wolfensberger, W. and Glenn, L. (1975) *PASS 3: Program Analysis of Service Systems*, Toronto: G. Allan Roeher Institute.

Wolfensberger, W. and Thomas, S. (1983) *PASSING: Program Analysis of Service Systems Implementation of Normalisation Goals*, Toronto: G. Allan Roeher Institute.

Yates, J. (1987) *Why Are We Waiting?: An Analysis of Hospital Waiting Lists*, Oxford: Oxford University Press.

Zeithaml, V.A., Berry, L.L. and Parasuraman, A. (1988) Communication and control processes in the delivery of service quality. *Journal of Marketing*, **52**, April: 35–48.

Zeithaml, V.A., Parasuraman, A. and Berry, L.L. (1990) *Delivering Quality Service: Balancing Customer Perceptions and Expectations*, New York, NY: Free Press.

INDEX

THE WILEY SERIES IN CLINICAL PSYCHOLOGY

Series Editors

Fraser N. Watts   *MRC Applied Psychology, Unit,*
                            Cambridge, UK

J. Mark G. Williams   *Department   of   Psychology,   University*
                            College of North Wales, Bangor, UK
                            continued from page ii

Edgar Miller and   The Psychology of Dementia
Robin Morris

Ronald Blackburn   The Psychology of Criminal Conduct:
                            Theory, Research and Practice

Ian H. Gotlib and   Psychological Aspects of Depression:
Constance L. Hammen   Toward a Cognitive-Interpersonal
                            Integration

Max Birchwood and   Innovations in the Psychological
Nicholas Tarrier (Editors) Management of Schizophrenia:
                            Assessment, Treatment and Services

Robert J. Edelmann   Anxiety: Theory, Research and
                            Intervention in Clinical and Health
                            Psychology

Alastair Ager (Editor)   Microcomputers and Clinical
                            Psychology: Issues, Applications and
                            Future Developments